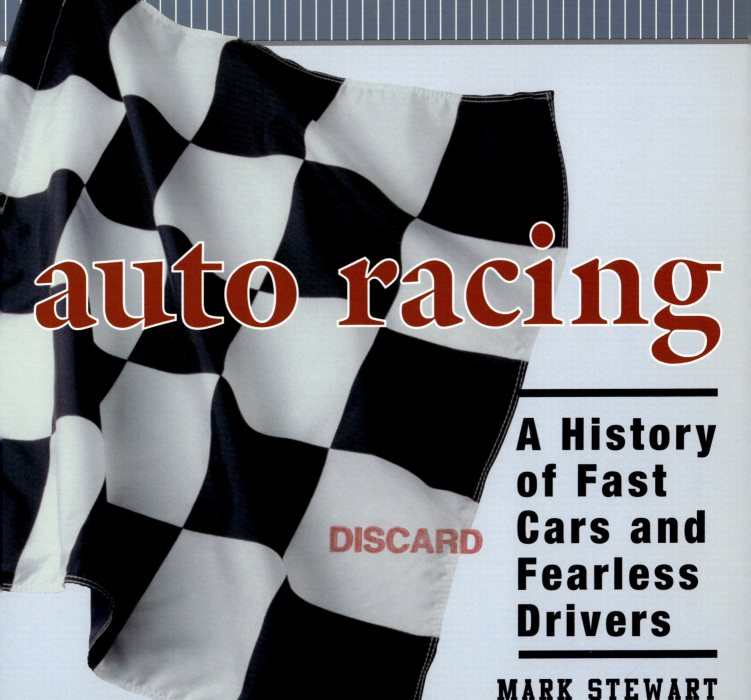

auto racing

A History of Fast Cars and Fearless Drivers

MARK STEWART

FRANKLIN WATTS
A Division of Grolier Publishing
New York • London • Hong Kong • Sydney
Danbury, Connecticut

Cover design by Dave Klaboe   Series design by Molly Heron
Research by Mike Kennedy
Photographs © Allsport USA: 6 bottom, 17, 32 (Hulton Getty), 66 bottom, 94 (Ken Levine), 59 (MSI), 95 (Jamie Squire), 79 (Vandystad); AP/Wide World Photos: cover bottom right, 92 top (Phil Coale), 89 (Amy Sancetta), 73, 74, 85 top; Archive Photos: 88 (Reuters/Renzo Gostoli), 19 (Ingram Collection), 92 bottom (Reuters/ Karl Ronstrom), 75; Brown Brothers: cover top center, 6 top, 22, 38; Corbis-Bettmann: 56 (Reuters), 20, 26, 27, 33, 44, 55 (UPI), 5, 12, 30; Daytona Racing Archive: cover top left, 40, 48, 52, 54, 63, 64, (International Speedway Corporation/NASCAR); IMS Properties, Inc.: cover top right, cover center middle, 42, 58, 60, 81 top (Indy 500 Photos), 81 bottom (Leigh Spargur), 25, 90; Sports Illustrated Picture Collection: 85 bottom (Heinz Kluetmeier), 83 (Time Inc./George Tiedemann), 66 top (Time Inc./Neil Leifer), cover center right, 71 (Time, Inc./Tony Duffy); Team Stewart, Inc.: 37 (1957 Time Inc.), 39 (1965 Heathrow House), 43, 57, 70 (1977 Edito-Service S.A., Geneva), 72 (1983 The New York Times Book Co., Inc.), cover center left, 51 (1957 Southern Card and Novelty, Co.), 65 (Sports Illustrated 1961), cover bottom left, 15; Tom Burnside Motorsport Archive: 45, 67.

Visit Franklin Watts on the Internet at:

http://publishing.grolier.com

Stewart, Mark
     Auto racing: a history of fast cars and fearless drivers / Mark Stewart.
     p. cm. — (The Watts history of sports)
     Includes bibliographical references (p.) and index.
     Summary: Discusses the origins and evolution of automobile racing,
               as well as important events and key personalities
               in the history of this competitive pastime.
     ISBN 0-531-11491-0
     1. Automobile racing—History—Juvenile literature.
     [1. Automobile racing—History.] I. Title II. Series.
     GV1029.15.S85 1998
     796.72'09—dc21   98-25040
                                                                      CIP
                                                                      AC

Library of Congress Cataloging-in-Publication Data
© 1998 by Mark Stewart

All rights reserved. Published simultaneously in Canada

Printed in the United States of America

1 2 3 4 5 6 7 8 9 10 R 07 06 05 04 03 02 01 00 99

CONTENTS

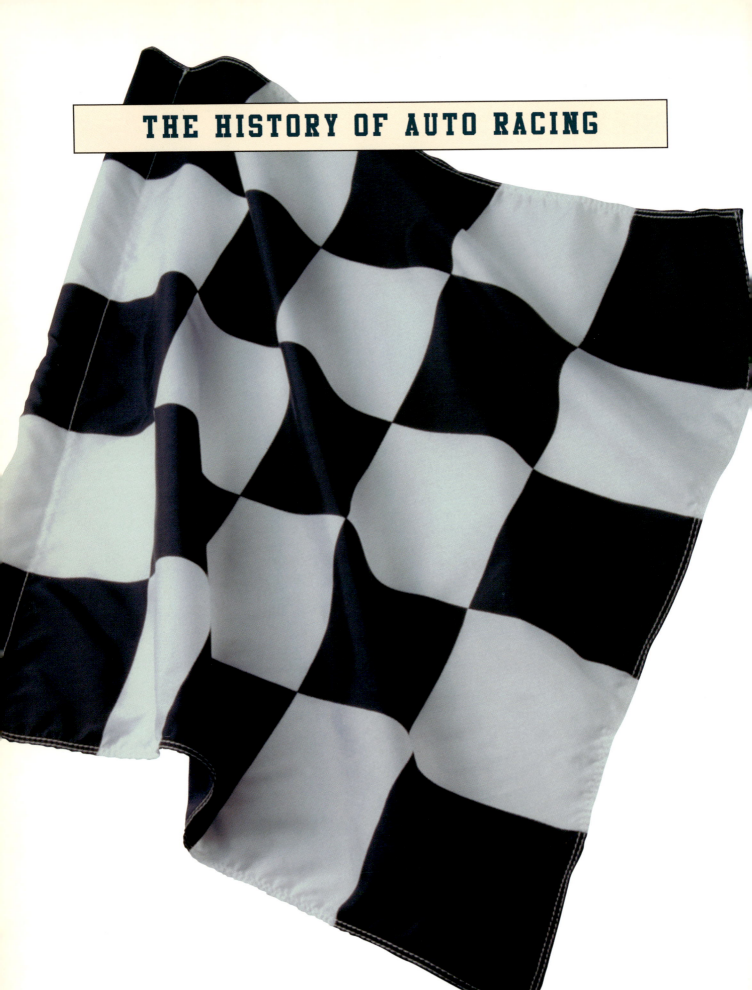

THE HISTORY OF AUTO RACING

The Birth of the Automobile

When the great inventions of the 19th century are discussed, the first ones that come to mind are the steam engine, electric lighting, and the telephone. These technologies transformed day-to-day life so profoundly that it is almost impossible to imagine living without them. But the invention that truly captured the imagination of people the world over was the automobile. In an age when everyone was looking toward the horizon and wondering what mysteries and adventures lay beyond it, the "horseless carriage" made pursuing the answers possible.

Freedom was the promise of the automobile. A person in a motor car could go anywhere he desired, any time he felt like it—at least in theory. Yet to a special breed of daredevils and dreamers, the real allure of the automobile was speed. Almost from the moment the first cars were available, there were people willing to risk their lives pushing these fragile machines to go farther and faster. Initially, they were merely the test pilots for the engineers and mechanics who sought to achieve a perfect balance between performance and reliability. But within just a few years, the men driving the cars developed a large and enthusiastic following all their own. Through these individuals people could experience the thrill of speed without the danger, and by rooting them on feel a part of an extraordinary revolution.

Thus a special bond developed between drivers and fans—one that would only grow stronger as the limits of speed and endurance were pushed further and further with each generation. Ultimately, this connection would prove one of the driving forces behind the evolution of the automobile, and spawn the most widespread and varied sport in the world.

The first car powered by an engine was demonstrated in the fall of 1863 by Etienne Lenoir in Paris, France. This touched off two decades of tinkering and experimentation that resulted in the internal combustion engine, which was invented by German engineer Karl Benz. He sold his first car, which had a top speed of 10 mph, to Frenchman Emile Roger, in 1888. In the interim, most car builders had been working with the steam engine, and the first motor race, held in Paris in 1887, was won by

Karl Benz, seated in an automobile he built in 1885. Benz sold his first car in 1888, about three decades before this picture was taken.

Count Jules de Dion, the noted sportsman who helped to pioneer auto racing in France

representing vehicles of every size and description. Some were powered by steam, others by gas, and several more used compressed air. A few claimed to use gravity or "pendulum power," while others were simply described as being "automatic." To separate the pretenders from the contenders, all entries first had to complete a 50-mile course in under four hours. This reduced the field considerably. On July 22, 21 cars lined up in Paris and, at 30-second intervals, roared off toward Rouen, some 80 miles away.

Of the 13 gas-powered cars, 5 were manufactured by Peugeot and 4 were made by Panhard-Levassors—both well-known and highly respected manufacturers. Much was at stake in this race. There was not yet a consensus of opinion regarding the merits

The first Panhard-Levassor, built in 1890. Designer Emile Levassor is seated at far right.

Count Jules de Dion, driving a steam-powered "quadricycle." The event was held by *Le Velocipede,* a publication devoted to racing of all kinds, and the Count was the only person to enter. Despite this lack of competition, there was no lack of enthusiasm for auto racing in France. Over the next few years the country would literally give birth to the sport, whereas many other European countries actually outlawed racing.

The First Races

In 1894, an exhibition run from Paris to Rouen was sponsored by *Le Petit Journal,* with the express purpose of generating positive publicity for the motor car. This event is considered to be the first modern automobile race. More than 100 entries were filed, of gas versus steam, and at the time steam-powered automobiles were much better negotiating hills. Behind the wheel of the lead car was the Count de Dion. A wealthy playboy who lived life on the edge, he was renowned for his skill as a gambler and had even fought the occasional duel. He was driving a steam-powered tractorlike vehicle with rubber tires up front and steel tires in the rear. The Count pulled away from his gas-powered competitors and chugged off through the French countryside. Each time he passed through a village, residents cheered and tossed flowers. The race was halted in the town of Mantes after 30 miles so the drivers could have lunch, which was something of a race in itself. The Count, however, took his time, and was the last to leave. Within 15 miles, however, he was back in the lead. De Dion encountered trouble along the way (spectators had to give him a push when his car got stuck in loose gravel, and at one point he took a wrong turn into a potato field), but still finished ahead of the pack, pulling into Rouen in a total time of 6 hours and 48 minutes. A Peugeot driven by Georges Lemaitre arrived a few minutes later, and another Peugeot finished third. One of the Panhards, with Emile Levassor at the wheel, finished fourth.

Although Jules de Dion had the fastest car, the "winner" of the event was Lemaitre. The Count was disqualified because his engine had to be stoked in order to finish, whereas the gas-powered cars were able to complete the 80 miles on a single tank of fuel. The Count was officially recognized as having the fastest car, but the Peugeots and Panhards split the 5,000-franc first prize for their excellent handling, safety, and overall performance.

The Paris-to-Rouen event was a pivotal moment in auto-racing history. It brought together Europe's most imaginative and skilled automobile enthusiasts, and created strong public demand for a race determined solely by the speed of the cars. A connection between spectators and drivers was also made that day. The throng lining the roadway was not cheering for the manufacturer when a car rumbled by—people were cheering for the man behind the wheel.

Four months later, de Dion invited Levassor, Robert Peugeot, and other key players in the fledgling automobile industry to his home in Paris. There they decided to stage a 732-mile competition in 1895 from Paris to Bordeaux and back again. The first car to cross the finish line would be the winner. The sport of auto racing was born.

News of the Paris-Bordeaux-Paris race spread across the globe. In the United States, where only a handful of Americans had even seen a motor car, millionaire William Vanderbilt and newspaper publisher James Gordon Bennett agreed to put up a large portion of the prize money, which totaled nearly 70,000 francs by the time the race started. There were 22 entries—13 gas-powered, 6 steam-powered, 1 electric, and a couple of motorcycles. The rules dictated that repairs could only be made with tools and parts carried onboard, and furthermore that each vehicle had to carry three or more passengers. Of course, no motorcycle carried three people; several of the cars also failed to meet this requirement. Manufacturers knew that the prestige and publicity would go to whoever crossed the finish line first, regardless of the rules; huge financial rewards were at stake.

As expected, the Count de Dion sped off to a substantial lead in his steam-powered vehicle, with another steam car following close behind. Both broke down early in the race, relinquishing the lead to a Panhard-Levassor driven by Levassor himself. Driving all night with a portable oil lamp lighting his way, Levassor averaged about 15 mph. He arrived in Ruffec, where a relief driver was supposed to be waiting, a few hours before dawn, but found the driver dead asleep. So Levassor decided to continue on himself. He reached Bordeaux at 10:40 A.M. and turned back for Paris with a three-and-a-half-hour lead on the Peugeots behind him. By this time he was feeling like a part of the machine, so when he churned into Ruffec on the way to Paris he did not stop for his driver. As Levassor neared Paris, word had spread throughout the city of his amazing feat. No one had ever driven this far or this long, let alone stayed at the wheel without a rest. When he arrived at the finish line, a huge crowd awaited him, and he was greeted like a conquering hero. In all, half of the vehicles that started the race reached Bordeaux, with a total of nine making it back to Paris.

In 1896, the Automobile Club of France—an organization created by Count Jules de Dion—announced an event covering more than 1,000 miles, from Paris to the southern seaport of Marseilles and back. To avoid night driving, the race was divided into 10 daylight-only stages. Among the hazards faced by the drivers were a terrible October rainstorm, fallen trees, and a bull with a definite dislike of motorized vehicles. As anticipated, Levassor forged an early lead, but was thrown from his car when it hit

MERRY OLD ENGLAND

British auto racing would have a long and glorious history, but it got off to a rather shaky start. Despite the popularity of autos among the well-to-do in England, racing on public roads was strictly forbidden. And those who owned motorized vehicles were not allowed to drive unless a man jogged ahead of the car with a red flag to warn horses and pedestrians. In August 1896, a woman was run down by a Benz outside of the Crystal Palace, becoming the first pedestrian fatality in the history of automobiles. In November of that same year, the first auto insurance policy was written. It covered the driver for damage and injury caused by accident, but specifically excluded any damage done by frightened horses.

Despite these hurdles, a 90-mile noncompetitive tour was staged from London to Brighton in November 1896. Emile Levassor was on hand in his Panhard, as were the three Bollee brothers, whose steam-powered tricycles had become quite popular in France. Although this was not officially a race, the 33 entrants were all trying to beat everyone to Brighton. Amedee Bollee finished first, just ahead of one of his siblings, Camille.

a dog and rolled over. He lay in an Avignon hospital bed while 13 other drivers (out of an original 32) continued on to Marseilles. The howling wind that had slowed them down on their way south pushed them toward Paris as they headed north. Levassor's factory assistant, a man by the name of Mayade, was the eventual winner.

The first steam-driven car to win a race was built by de Dion. It was driven by a friend of Count de Dion's, Count Gaston de Chasseloup-Laubat, in an 1897 race along the Mediterranean from Marseilles to Nice. This race was doubly significant, for it featured several cars modified specifically for racing. Most of the drivers had stripped off anything that added weight or drag to their automobiles, and several entrants had convinced car-makers to install more powerful engines than were available to the general public. Later in the year, another short sprint was held from Paris to Dieppe. Once race officials had seen to an orderly start, they boarded a special train to the finish line. The train was delayed and the drivers kept up a steady pace of around 20 to 25 mph, which put the first few finishers across the line before the officials could make it there. The car-beats-train story was the talk of Paris for weeks.

America Takes Notice

In the United States, interest in the automobile was starting to build. Encouraged by the success of the 1895 Paris-Bordeaux race, H. H. Kohlsaat, who owned the *Chicago Times-Herald,* announced his paper would sponsor a race on November 2, 1895, from Jackson Park north to Evanston and back. He received almost 100 entry applications for the event, and the entrants worked feverishly through the summer and fall to build their cars. Unfortunately, only two cars showed up for the race, so it was postponed until the 28th and as luck would have it a major snowstorm dumped a foot of powder on the city. Still, five automobiles arrived at the starting line and the race went on as planned. A sixth car got stuck in slush prior to the start and withdrew. Early in the race, a Macy-Benz driven by Jerry O'Connor collided with a horse-drawn bus, careened over railroad tracks and slammed into a sleigh carrying a group of journalists. Despite a damaged steering mechanism, O'Connor soon managed to take the lead. Right behind O'Connor was a Duryea Motor Wagon driven by Frank Duryea, and when the Macy-Benz's steering finally gave out on the way back to Chicago, Duryea puttered past him and into the lead. Duryea crossed the finish line after dark, and only a few dozen spectators remained from an original throng of hundreds. Duryea was awarded $2,000 as the first winner of an American road race. In second place was Oscar Mueller, driving the Mueller-Benz his father designed. Actually, an umpire guided the car across the finish line. Mueller had passed out from the cold.

Despite the weather problems and the lack of entries, the Chicago race was a grand success for Kohlsaat. Throughout the summer and fall, and especially in the days surrounding the race, Chicagoans bought the *Times-Herald* in record numbers. Americans were fascinated by the automobile, and hungered for information on the cars and drivers. With auto racing a proven circulation-booster, other publications began to look at the idea of staging major races. Toward the end of May 1896, *Cos-*

THE FIRST FATALITY

An 1898 event in southern France produced auto racing's first fatality. A driver named de Montariol, at the controls of a light Benz Parisienne, heard a bigger, faster Landrey-et-Beyroux coming up behind him and pulled over to the right to let it go by. The Landrey's driver, the Marquis de Montaignac—a friend of de Montariol—waved as he sped by but, in doing so, he let go of his steering tiller. The Landrey veered into the Benz and forced it up and over an embankment. De Montariol was okay, but his mechanic's head was crushed under the weight of the car. The Marquis turned and watched in horror, then his own car went up the same embankment and rolled into the same field. He and his mechanic were badly injured and both died a short time later.

mopolitan organized a 104-mile event with a $3,000 first prize. Of the six cars that started, only three made it out of Manhattan, and all three failed to make it up Ardsley Hill in Westchester. Members of a nearby country club came over and pushed the three cars up the hill, and they proceeded to Irvington-on-Hudson, where they wheeled around and headed back to the city. Frank Duryea won the event to become the first two-time champion in auto-racing history.

Later that fall, the organizers of the Rhode Island State Fair held an event on a one-mile, dirt horse-racing track, marking the first automobile race on a closed circuit. This proved an immensely popular idea, for it enabled fans to watch a race from start to finish. It also pleased promoters, who were able to charge admission to the 50,000 spectators who showed up. The payoff from Duryea's two victories was evident already, as five of the cars entered in Rhode Island had been purchased from his company. But

this time it was an electric car that won, a Riker driven by designer A. L. Riker.

These races stirred up interest among wealthy sportsmen, and led to more competition—and car-building—over the next few years. But by 1900 it was becoming evident that the United States was lagging behind in automotive design and manufacturing. That year, James Gordon Bennett, publisher of the *New York Herald,* decided to finance an international event. He hoped that it might light a fire underneath American automakers, and stimulate the industry in other countries besides France, which produced the world's two fastest brands in Panhard and Mors. Bennett dictated that only three cars from each country could enter his race, and that they had to be manufactured entirely in their country of origin. Also, a country's automobile club—not its manufacturers—would determine which cars and drivers should enter the race.

The first Gordon Bennett Race was to take place in France, with succeeding races to be held in the country that won the previous year's title. Despite the location of the first race, Bennett's rules were decidedly anti-French. France could have put a dozen cars and drivers in the field, as opposed to most of the other interested nations, which would have trouble getting even one car to the starting line. France won the race as expected, with a Panhard driven by François Charron limping home after hitting a dog 10 miles from the finish.

Paris to Amsterdam

Although the shorter races held in 1896 and 1897 were popular with spectators and drivers, the manufacturers preferred longer races. In a 50- or 100-mile event anyone could win. In a 500-mile or 1,000-mile competition, however, the best cars were going to triumph. And the car builders knew that winning such a race would sell a lot of product. Of course, they recognized their customers were not going to enter their cars in road races, but wealthy people—at that time the whole of the car-buying public— wanted to be associated with a winner.

With so many potential customers at stake, manufacturers began making road races the ultimate proving ground for all variety of engineering and design ideas. With the goal of making a faster, more responsive, and more reliable car than anyone else's, the car companies competed furiously to come up with the best designs and innovations, and during the years prior to 1900 several important advances were made. The two-cylinder engines that powered the first racing cars were doubled up and converted to four-cylinder models, and horsepower soared. Where only a few years earlier drivers had struggled to push their

cars above 25 mph, now the 50-mph barrier was ready to fall.

Other innovations from this period that remain a part of today's automobiles include Panhard-Levassor's gill-tubed radiator, designed to keep engines cool. The company also was one of the first to switch from a tiller to a steering wheel, which was copied almost instantly by everyone in the business. Edouard Michelin, whose pneumatic (air-filled) tires gave a much smoother ride than solid rubber models, finally hit upon a reliable design after testing out various theories under racing conditions.

In the summer of 1898, the big event all the manufacturers wanted was finally held. A race from Paris to Amsterdam and back would cover nearly 900 miles and give the industry exposure in France, Belgium, Luxembourg, and Holland. Four dozen automobiles started the race, and it was close all the way. The pack reached Amsterdam and turned home for Paris, with Fernand Charron (a former bicycle racer) holding a slim lead in his brightly painted Panhard. Right behind him was Leonce Girardot in another Panhard, with Francois Giraud, in a Bollee, ready to take the lead if they faltered. On the final day, the race was decided by flat tires—always a problem on the dirt roads of the day. Girardot had fewer than Charron and passed him to cross the finish line first, but the big winner was Panhard-Levassor, with the top two cars in the most ambitious race ever held. Sales went through the roof in France, and orders for the company's cars poured in from all over Europe.

The 1898 season saw the birth of another important part of auto racing: pure speed. In December, *La France Automobile* magazine held an event where cars were

Camille Jenatzy, seated in his battery-powered Jamais Contente, in the spring of 1899. Believing that electric cars had reached their peak, Jenatzy switched to gas-powered models. He won the 1903 Gordon Bennett race in a Mercedes.

timed over a straight, two-kilometer course. Count de Chasseloup-Laubat won the race in an electric car with a speed of 39.3 mph. A well-known driver by the name of Camille Jenatzy challenged the Count to a "duel," and the first "drag race" was scheduled for early 1899. A large and enthusiastic crowd showed up to witness this event, which saw the challenger turn in a speed of 41 mph. The Count, who had been tinkering with his engine since his 1898 victory, shot down the course at an unprecedented speed, but his engine blew before he reached the finish line. He had built up enough momentum to coast the final 200 meters and still

beat Jenatzy with a speed of 43.7 mph. Reaction to this race was unprecedented. Fans demanded more, and 10 days later the two drivers met again. This time Jenatzy became the first to reach 50 mph, while de Chasseloup-Laubat's engine burned out at the starting line. In March they met for a third time and the Count roared home with a speed of 57.6 mph. Jenatzy decided to go after the record on his own from there, and in a car he named Jamais Contente (Never Satisfied) wowed spectators by going 65 mph.

Jenatzy's electric car might have been the fastest in the world, but battery-powered automobiles were beginning to fade from the scene. By the turn of the century gas-powered engines were proving to be the best. On paper, their power could be increased mightily without a dramatic increase in size. By contrast, steam engines—their main competition—would become too large and difficult to operate as the public demanded more and more speed. In the real world, internal combustion engines were already producing up to 20 horsepower—more than triple that achieved just a few years before. Indeed, the 1895 Paris-Bordeaux-Paris race, which had taken more than two days to complete, could now be run in a single day. And longer races—such as the 1898 Paris-Amsterdam-Paris race and the 1,378-mile "Tour de France," held in 1899—could be held in a week.

Speeding into the 20th Century

The Gordon Bennett competition was just one of many races which sought to involve other countries. In 1901, a three-day race was held from Paris to Berlin, Germany. The winner was Henri Fournier, who had been Fernand Charron's co-driver in the first Gordon Bennett victory. More than 20,000 spectators were at the finish line to greet Fournier, which showed clearly that there were plenty of auto-racing fans outside of France. This race was also notable for its problems. Racing cars were becoming so big and powerful that the drivers sometimes could not control them, and there were several crashes that were directly related to this situation. Also, a little boy was killed; he darted into the road to watch a car as it disappeared down the road and seconds later was run over by another car,

which emerged out of the cloud of dust the first car had left behind. This incident was the last straw for the French government, which had been fielding complaints from those who claimed that manufacturers were no longer building racing cars to advertise their touring models, but just to win races. Given that dozens of people had already been injured when cars careened into crowds at other races, the government issued a ban on road races of any kind. A final race from Paris to Vienna, Austria, was allowed early in 1902, and that was it for the year.

The year 1902 saw an interesting concept debut in Belgium, where a 318-mile race was held not from one city to another, but on a 53-mile course that wound through the Ardennes Forest near Bastogne. That same year, the Gordon Bennett Race was won by an Englishman, Selwyn Edge, who drove a Napier. This touched off a public cry for the legalization of road racing in Great Britain, where it had long been outlawed. Edge had won the Gordon Bennett race for England, and fans meant to see it run on their soil in 1903. It took an act of Parliament to okay a closed-course competition in a sparsely populated section of Ireland.

The makeup of the German team for the Gordon Bennett hinted at a subtle change in the sport. Mercedes entered two test drivers from their manufacturing plant, Otto Hieronymus and Christian Werner, feeling that as employees they were the best people to drive its cars. A problem arose when it was pointed out that they were not members of their country's automobile club, which was for wealthy "sportsmen," not lowly factory workers. Clearly, this point would have to be addressed, and sooner rather than later. As it turned out, the cars Mercedes meant to enter were lost in a factory fire, and replaced with three stripped-down machines, with three new drivers. Jenatzy—not a German but a Belgian—was one of the new men, and he drove to victory with three Frenchmen on his tail.

Meanwhile, road racing returned briefly to France in 1903, with disastrous consequences. With speeds now approaching 100 mph, the public demanded to see its top cars and drivers going full-out through the French countryside. Eventually, the government gave in. There had been no fatalities in the lone 1902 race, and King Alfonso of neighboring Spain put his considerable influence behind the race, which would start in Paris and end in Madrid. Three million people lined the route—100,000 of whom were in Paris to witness the biggest starting field ever. More than 200 cars of varying weight and power roared off the line, along with 59 motorcycles. The combination of heavy traffic, high speed, and dirt roads, however, proved disastrous. Before the race even reached Bordeaux, several cars hit trees or rolled into ditches and open fields. Four drivers—including Marcel Renault—and two spectators were killed, and several more people were badly injured.

Appalled at the carnage, officials from the French and Spanish governments agreed to stop the race. This time there was little complaining from the fans or the auto manufacturers—given the present set of conditions, racing cars had evolved beyond man's ability to control them. This feeling was echoed throughout Europe, and what racing was allowed to continue was tightly controlled. No more would vehicles of different weight classes be permitted in the same race, and rather than plotting courses

through heavily populated areas, officials began looking for remote locales. Those who had opposed racing from the beginning were now being heard, and some even went as far as to scatter nails in front of drivers when races went through their towns.

With nothing going on in France in 1904, the two big races in Europe were the Gordon Bennett and Belgium's Circuit des Ardennes. The former, which the Germans made into nothing short of a national holiday, was a huge success. The latter was won by George Heath, an American-born tailor who had taken up residence in Paris.

As the first American to win a European event, Heath was hailed as a conquering hero when he returned to the U.S. to compete in the Vanderbilt Cup, the newest race on the international scene. It was sponsored by young millionaire William Vanderbilt, who was an accomplished driver himself. Vanderbilt had finished third in the 1902 Circuit des Ardennes and briefly held the world speed record. He had seen what big races had done for automobile manufacturing in Europe and, like Bennett, wanted American companies to catch up. The rules were more or less the same as the Gordon Bennett, with a stipulation that the race remain in the United States for at least two years.

The first Vanderbilt Cup—America's first international auto race—was held in Long Island on October 8, 1904. It comprised 10 laps of a 28.4-mile course, and featured 18 entries. Only five of the cars were American-made (although most of the drivers were American), and were little more than stripped-down showroom cars—nothing like the specialized racers from France, Italy, and Germany. Heath, driving a French Panhard similar to the one he had

George Robertson speeds through a turn on the final lap of the 1908 Vanderbilt Cup. Robertson finished first despite tire trouble (in this photo he has just one spare left). His Locomobile was the first American car to win the race.

in Belgium, managed to take and hold the lead. Eighty-eight seconds later, Frenchman Albert Clement, driving a Clement-Bayard, crossed the finish line. The crowd, unschooled in the finer points of auto racing, swarmed onto the track to congratulate the winner, just as they might at the finish of a baseball or football game. Needless to say, none of the other drivers were able to finish the race.

The Vanderbilt Cup proved to be a success. It grabbed headlines and captured the imagination of sports fans, who represented a fast-growing segment of the American middle class. Prior to this event, auto racing in the U.S. had been confined primarily to country fairs and sporting clubs, and had almost no impact on automakers. One-mile dirt tracks had been operating outside of

New York City in Yonkers and Brighton Beach, but had failed to generate interest outside the immediate region. Automaker Henry Ford had seen the connection between speed and car sales, and actually broke the world record with an elaborately staged demonstration behind the wheel of his Ford Arrow on a frozen lake near his Detroit manufacturing plant. But not until an American driver beat the Europeans on American soil (albeit in a French car) did the sport begin to take off in the States. Over the next few years, as Americans grew to accept and then romanticize the automobile, the relationship between car design and auto racing became quite strong. Soon, auto racing in the United States would take on a life of its own, and assume a very special place in American culture.

In 1905, the Automobile Club of France, still bristling at what it felt was America's undue influence over European racing, made a move to abolish the Gordon Bennett in favor of its own race, which it called the Grand Prix (Grand Prize). The magazine *L'Auto* supported this idea, and promised to put up a truly grand prize of 100,000 francs, but complaints from other countries forced France to shelve this idea. The Gordon Bennett went on as scheduled, with Frenchman Leon Thery winning on his home soil. The big surprise in this race, however, was the performance of the Italians. Vincenzo Lancia, driving one of Italy's three 110-horsepower Fiats, briefly held the lead, and at one point he and teammates Alessandro Cagno and Felice Nazzaro were running 2-3-4 behind Thery. Lancia's first lap was the fastest in the entire race.

The Italians earned so much respect from their performance that several French drivers made immediate plans to enter the Coppa Florio, held in northern Italy. To their astonishment, this event was won by an Italian amateur, driving an Itala. At the second Vanderbilt Cup, Vincenzo Lancia had the race all but won when American Walter Christie, in his front-wheel drive Christie, smashed into him on a curve. The ensuing delay enabled Victor Hemery to win the race in a French Darracq. More than 200,000 people made their way to Long Island to witness the race, and local potato farmers charged up to $50 for prime viewing locations.

Auto racing was now well-established in the United States, Great Britain, France, Belgium, Austria, Germany, and Italy. In just a decade, every aspect of auto racing—from organization to technology to public interest—had grown by great leaps and bounds, making the sport the most sophisticated and exciting in the world. As the industrial age neared its zenith, racing represented the ultimate marriage of human beings and technology. It also held up a mirror to this relationship, asking that most compelling question: Who is actually in control, man or machine?

Grand Prix Racing Arrives

Most of the different types of auto racing that exist today can be traced back to an important split in philosophy that occurred in 1906. The French were successful in dumping the Gordon Bennett race in favor of their Grand Prix, removing American influence from European racing and enabling the Automobile Club of France to set its own course. Although there was no chance the government would ever again permit the dangerous city-to-city races French manufacturers loved so much, their thirst for distance was adequately quenched by the new Grand Prix, which could be run on a course almost as long and challenging as the old races.

The first Grand Prix was held west of the town of Le Mans, whose city fathers put up a bundle of cash to persuade the Automobile Club of France to plan the 60-mile circuit nearby. To avoid the tragedies of the past, roads were improved, grandstands constructed, and wooden fencing erected to keep spectators off the track. In areas where roads were especially dangerous, wooden planks were laid to provide a negotiable surface. The race was a 12-lap affair, conducted over two days, and there were no fatalities. However, the tar spread over the roads to improve traction began to break up

Three of auto racing's early stars competed in the 1906 French Grand Prix. Felice Nazzaro (left) finished second in a Fiat; Francois Szisz (center) won the race in a Renault; Albert Clement, in a car of his own design, placed third.

in the June sun, pummeling drivers and mechanics when they came up behind another car, and shredding tires. The race, in fact, was decided on tire changes, as conditions worsened on the second day. Francois Szisz won in his Renault, which had detachable rims devised by Michelin. He saved 10 minutes per tire change over his competitors, and won by 32 minutes. Sales of Renault cars nearly doubled that year, and tripled over a two-year period. Fiat, whose car came in second, also saw sales skyrocket. Both Peugeot and Fiat made smaller cars with the same user-friendly Michelin tire system. They were closer to what people were actually buying, and sales no doubt benefited from this.

This relationship was not lost on European manufacturers, but they were hesitant to pour research and development efforts into smaller, more efficient cars that would get blown away by the monstrous French machines. What began to happen in each country was that manufacturers started pressuring their national auto clubs to create races that favored the types of cars they wished to produce. In Italy, this meant mountain races that favored the Fiats and Isotta-Fraschinis and weighed against the French. In Germany, races were held with limits on engine size and car weight, which also cut the big French cars out of the picture and favored cars made by Benz, Mercedes, and Opel. In England, where road racing was still illegal, a kidney-shaped concrete track—the first of its kind in the world—was constructed near London in the town of Brooklands.

Slowly but surely, the center of the auto-racing world began to shift away from France and toward Italy, where its cars consistently outperformed the competition in the big events, and Felice Nazzaro became his country's first great driver.

Birth of the Brickyard

One of the disturbing trends in the automotive industry, besides the increasing size of engines, was the flimsy frames on which they were mounted. It was a classic example of two wrongs not making a right, as designers took the easy way out. Making a bigger, heavier engine was the simple way to get more power, and compensating for all that weight with a fragile, stripped-down chassis was careless and stupid. Each country tried to restrict this practice, but that led to a lot of confusion, so in 1907 an international commission set a standard "formula" that everyone could follow. It limited the size of engines and set a minimum weight so that designers would no longer be compelled to construct fragile chassis.

In the United States, this led to a new race and a sudden shift in power. The Vanderbilt Cup, which was run by the American Automobile Association, ignored the new formula, which drew strong complaints from European manufacturers. The Automobile Club of America, which was run by wealthy auto enthusiasts, had always felt that it should control the sport, and it seized this opportunity to create a race called the American Grand Prize, to be run on a 25-mile course in Savannah, Georgia, on Thanksgiving Day. The response was overwhelming, as Europe sent its top cars and drivers to the U.S. The crowd watched in awe as the greatest names in the sport jockeyed for position in an intensely close six-hour race. Louis Wagner, a French driver behind the wheel of a German Benz, finished first in a race that showcased Benzes and Italian Fiats. No French cars were ever in contention, and of the six American-made cars that started the race, not a single one was able to finish. Henry Ford, whose factory had just started mass-producing Model Ts, realized that American cars would never seriously compete on the international level until the manufacturers stopped trying to modify stock cars and started designing racing cars.

That did not mean the racing business was suffering. On the contrary, Americans could not get enough of the sport. It seemed that anywhere someone carved out a dirt oval and constructed grandstands, a large and enthusiastic crowd was guaranteed to show up. Ford's Model T—the first automobile that the average person could afford—sparked a national fascination with the automobile that spread like wildfire.

One of the millions of Americans intrigued by the auto was a businessman from Indiana named Carl Fisher, who owned the Prest-O-Lite headlamp company. He and his partner, James Allison, joined forces with Arthur Newby of National Motors and Frank Wheeler, who owned a company that manufactured carburetors. The four entrepreneurs believed, as did Ford, that the U.S. auto industry would have to start producing race cars that could compete anywhere in the world. And to do that, they would need a proving ground. They pooled their resources, bought a large parcel of land in Indianapolis for $250,000, built a rectangular track with rounded corners, and named it the Indianapolis Motor Speedway. The group felt that the burgeoning U.S. auto industry would pay to use the track to test all of its vehicles—both commercial and competitive—and they also put a plan into motion to stage a automobile race.

That first race was held in August 1909, and it was every bit as successful as Fisher and his partners had hoped. People came from hundreds of miles around to witness the event, which was won by Louis Schwitzer in a Stoddard Dayton. The race was a two-lap sprint around the 2.5-mile track. One major problem arose, however, and that was the material used to pave the track. The surface was made of crushed stone over tar, and it simply did not hold up. Debris flew everywhere, and caused several crashes. A driver, two mechanics, and two spectators were killed, and much criticism was leveled at the Speedway's owners. They responded by ripping up the surface and replacing it with 3 million 10-pound bricks (soon it would be known the world over as the "Brickyard"), and constructing retaining walls and guard rails to protect the fans.

The track reopened in May 1910, and 42 races were held over a three-day period. More races—from 10 to 200 miles—were held on July 4 and Labor Day. The surface proved itself worthy, the Speedway turned a handsome profit, and Fisher was back in the city's good graces. That fall, he began to think bigger. To make Indy the center of the American racing world, he would need to attract the biggest manufacturers and best drivers in racing. To do that, he would have to give them a reason to come. That winter he announced a 500-mile race to be held on Memorial Day, with a purse of more than $27,000. When the green flag dropped on the first Indianapolis 500, 40 cars roared across the starting line as 77,000 fans roared their approval.

A truck advertises the "World's Greatest Auto Races" at Carl Fisher's Indianapolis Motor Speedway. Within a few years, Fisher was delivering on this promise.

Ray Harroun speeds to victory in a Marmon Wasp at the first Indy 500 in 1911.

The Indianapolis Motor Speedway made auto racing understandable for a lot of sports fans who knew nothing of automobile designs. It also created America's first group of famous drivers. In the early years of Indy, the names and faces of Johnny Aitken, Bob Burman, Joe Dawson, Ray Harroun, Eddie Hearne, Barney Oldfield, and Howdy Wilcox became familiar to those who scanned the sports pages. Harroun won the first 500-mile race in a car built by the Indianapolis-based Marmon company. He had joined the company three years earlier as a test driver and engineer, and brought the company fame by winning the American National Championship in 1910. Harroun, who completed the race in 6 hours 42 minutes, was the only driver who went the 500 miles without a mechanic. His reputation made, he retired from racing, claiming the dangers of the profession were too great to make it a "career."

Although closed-track racing took a lot of the variables out of the mix, it did not diminish the dangers drivers faced. Hazards such as dogs, rough surfaces, and unexpected turns had been eliminated, but this just emboldened drivers to take curves faster and make riskier passes. There were just as many crashes and just as many racing deaths, yet there was never a shortage of drivers or racing fans. The danger actually seemed to attract them.

Hoping to seize on the success of Indy, the American Automobile Association began to sanction a series of similar races across the country. These events—most of which were run on dirt tracks or wooden "roaring board" surfaces—featured the same cars and drivers, but never came close to matching the popularity of the 500. Still, they did lay the foundation for future racing leagues, and helped determine the overall Indy car champion each year.

The international prestige of the Indy 500 grew quickly, as did the prize money for winning. In 1912, Joe Dawson took the checkered flag, though he led for only the last two laps of the race. The following year, Dawson failed to qualify. This was not a reflection on his skill, but on the state of the automotive industry in the United States. Henry Ford and other pioneers had succeeded in putting America behind a steering wheel, but they had made little progress in the area of racing engines. Europe first brought its pure racing cars to Indy in 1913, and these cars and drivers dominated. American cars had little chance against engines specifically designed to generate maximum horsepower under racing conditions—technologically, they still lagged behind their Old World competitors. Jules Goux, driving a Peugeot and downing three bottles of champagne, took the checkered flag to restore some dignity to France's tattered reputation. In 1914, French machines took the top four spots, and in 1915 Ralph DePalma—who had resigned from the Mercer team—drove a German Mercedes to victory. In 1916, Peugeot won again, with Dario Resta driving.

Peugeot Takes the Lead

The years preceding the First World War were rough ones for European racing. Grand Prix competition was struggling to retain popular support, and Europe was also going through an economic recession, which made staging big international events difficult. Racing began to shake off its malaise in 1911, when Robert Peugeot decided to do whatever it took for his company to regain the top spot in the automotive world. Jules Goux convinced him to manufacture his racing cars in a to-

tally separate factory, which was a revolutionary idea at the time.

Even more revolutionary was that this new manufacturing team would be headed by three drivers: Goux, Georges Baillot, and Paolo Zuccarelli. The senior designers at Peugeot laughed at this idea, but Peugeot knew what he was doing. Who better than a driver to determine how best to make a racing car faster and more durable? An added bonus was that Zuccarelli—a test driver for Peugeot during the company's glory years—had spent time in Spain with Hispano-Suiza, a highly regarded race-car manufacturer. These three then hired Ernest Henry, a Swiss engineer who had an extensive knowledge of combustion chambers and valve layout from his work with powerboats.

This was not a "Dream Team"—in fact, they were called "the Charlatans" by their critics. But in 1912, they turned out a car that represented a major breakthrough. It had a four-cylinder engine with four valves per cylinder, and an overhead camshaft design and hemispherical combustion chambers. The bottom line is that it was more powerful and efficient than anything that had ever been built, and it got automotive designers thinking in a whole new way.

In 1913, Peugeot dominated races on both sides of the Atlantic, and an L-76 driven by Goux traveled 106 miles in an hour to break a speed/distance record formerly set by an airplane. The longtime Peugeot driver won the Indianapolis 500, then returned to France for the Grand Prix. Sadly, Zuccarelli perished prior to the race, when he collided with a hay cart that unexpectedly crossed in front of him during a practice run. Baillot won the event and Goux finished second.

BARNEY AND RALPH

Barney Oldfield is considered by many historians to be America's first modern sports "superstar." At a time when the country was beginning to feel its true might, Oldfield embodied a lot of the qualities that excited people in the United States. He was the fastest, the bravest, and the brashest. He was obsessed with winning, and responded to any and all authority with open disdain.

Oldfield understood the immense potential of the automobile before most Americans had even seen one. In 1902, at the age of 24, he switched from bicycle racing to auto racing. Driving a Ford 999, he won his first race. A year later, Oldfield became the first U.S. driver to cover a mile in less than 60 seconds. It was at this time that his genius for self-promotion became apparent. Oldfield toured the nation as the famous "Mile-A-Minute" man and people flocked to see him. He survived countless crashes and set every imaginable speed record, from short distances to long road races. Driving with a cigar clenched between his teeth, Oldfield cut quite a figure in the daredevil days of racing.

Oldfield loved one-on-one match races, as did his fans. But the American Automobile Association saw these events as pure showmanship, and felt they impeded its attempt to organize racing. Oldfield was constantly under suspension by AAA, and barred from many of its official races. Still, he remained America's most popular driver. He would race anything—even tractors—if the money was right. And any time there were celebrities around, he made sure to have his photo snapped with them for the newspapers. Soon it was the celebrities who wanted their pictures snapped with Oldfield. He had become a larger-than-life figure in popular culture, and his name was a household word the way Babe Ruth's would be many years later. Oldfield was more than glitz, though. He

Barney Oldfield races against flier Lincoln Beachy in a 1910 contest.

worked hard to improve conditions in the sport and helped to create the first union for drivers.

By the mid-teens, his popularity was beginning to ebb. The success of the Indianapolis Motor Speedway signaled a new era in American racing, and there soon would be no room for mavericks like Oldfield. He retired in 1918, and took a position with Firestone Tire and Rubber, where he pioneered several ideas that contributed to driver safety. Oldfield continued to trade on his celebrity, and made millions during the 1920s. He continued his flamboyant lifestyle until the Great Depression wiped him out. Yet even in the 1930s and 1940s, he still was considered a celebrity of the first magnitude, and he managed to make a decent living as an engineering consultant and occasional guest speaker at special events.

When Oldfield was at the height of his popularity, another American driver began to grab fame by working within the system. Ralph DePalma was the top driver in AAA-sanctioned events, which made him the country's best driver, at least officially. Oldfield and DePalma were well aware of each other, but felt there was room enough for each to do his thing without impeding the other's progress. Thus while Oldfield was setting speed records and making headlines as he barnstormed from town to town, DePalma was winning hundreds of official races, and making plenty of headlines of his own. In 1912, for instance, he won the undying admiration of racing fans at the Indianapolis 500 when his car blew its oil and came to a stop a mile short of the finish line. DePalma, who was in the lead, refused to give up. He and his mechanic pushed the car the rest of the way to the wild cheering of the crowd. Although immediately disqualified, he became a bona fide legend that day.

Oldfield and DePalma finally crossed swords in 1914, when Oldfield was hired to drive for DePalma's Mercer team in the Vanderbilt Cup without consulting DePalma. DePalma resigned on the spot, and entered the race in an older Mercedes Grey Ghost. He and Oldfield ran a thrilling race, with Oldfield pulling ahead with just 10 laps to go. DePalma slowed down two laps later and signaled to his pit crew he was coming in. Oldfield decided he would pit, too, to change a worn tire. But DePalma never actually stopped, and managed to pull ahead before Oldfield realized he had been tricked. He sped off after DePalma and barely lost the race. From that day on the two were mortal enemies, and America had its first great auto racing rivalry.

DePalma never went back to Mercer, choosing instead to enter the Grey Ghost in other races, winning the 1915 Indy 500 and driving successfully well into the 1920s. Regardless of the car he was driving, DePalma was considered to be a factor in any race he entered. He was intelligent, confident, and knew every trick there was when it came to winning an automobile race. After DePalma "retired," he moved on to stock cars, where he became an influential figure during the rough-and-tumble early days of that sport.

By 1914, most of Europe's major automotive companies had adopted Peugeot's engine design. The Grand Prix, run in July, saw Mercedes sweep to victory before a stunned French crowd. A month later, Germany and France were at war, and the European automotive industry turned its attention toward national defense.

The First World War began to affect American racing in 1915, as there was a noticeable absence of new European automobiles and far fewer European drivers. But people like Carl Fisher saw the conflict abroad as a chance for American auto manufacturing to catch up. He ordered two 1914 Peugeots and sent them to Premier Motor so they could be dissected, analyzed, and ultimately copied. Meanwhile, long road races—a European specialty—began to lose favor with the public, and especially with promoters, who never found a good way to charge people for watching the contestants whiz by. Without the allure of the latest, greatest road racers from overseas, fan interest turned increasingly to events held on small oval tracks. This suited promoters just fine, and they built new wooden-surfaced "speedbowls" during 1915 and 1916 in major cities including Brooklyn, Chicago, Omaha, and Cincinnati. The AAA's National Championship, which was determined by points won in a combination of road and track races, reflected this change. In 1915, 10 road races were included, but in 1916 that number fell to two. By 1917, all AAA races were being held on one- and two-mile oval tracks.

Although the racing season was not shut down by the government during the war years of 1917 and 1918, it did slow considerably. Fisher decided to close down the 500 for those two years, turning the Speed-

way over to the military for vehicle and aircraft repairs and testing. Other races went on as scheduled, but the most important development during the war occurred in aircraft research and development. As the front bogged down in Europe, the role of airplanes became increasingly significant, and the U.S. government asked several car manufacturers to put their best people into engine development. Working with a 16-cylinder engine developed by Bugatti, noted racing enthusiast Charles King assembled some of the top minds in American automotive design, including Fred Duesenberg and carburetor pioneer Harry Miller. The war ended before they could produce more than one flying engine, but during their time together they had learned a tremendous amount about engine design. So had others in the industry, both in the U.S. and Europe. As the 1919 racing season got under way, some major changes were in the wind.

The 1920s

When the Armistice was signed in November 1918, the racing world was anxious to get back to business. A lot had changed since 1914. At Peugeot, Ernest Henry and a talented but inexperienced Italian engineer named Ettore Bugatti had seen the future, and it looked like an eight-cylinder, overhead camshaft engine. In America, Harry Miller and Fred Duesenberg had come to the same conclusion. By 1921 eight-cylinder cars were beginning to turn up in big races on both sides of the Atlantic.

This was also the year when international racing began to recapture its prewar vibrancy and glamour. The French Grand Prix was on again at Le Mans (German en-

tries were not welcome), while Italy staged the Targa Florio as well as six other major events. The Indianapolis 500, which had featured a mix of old and new vehicles in 1919 and 1920, was thoroughly up-to-date by 1921, with the top cars and competitors converging on the speedway from all corners of the racing world. There the Americans confirmed what many had been whispering since the war ended: the Yanks had not only caught up to the Europeans, they were now manufacturing superior automobiles. Louis Chevrolet entered a pair of eight-cylinder Frontenacs at Indy, and Duesenberg entered eight. A trio of eight-cylinder cars—designed for France's Ballot company by Henry—were the only threat to American dominance. Tommy Milton, driving one of the Chevys, edged Roscoe Sarles and his Duesenberg.

Fred Duesenberg hated to lose, and wanted desperately to run his cars at the French Grand Prix. Strapped for cash, he was unable to afford to make the race until he formed an alliance with French sparkplug manufacturer Albert Champion. Champion wired $60,000 to the U.S., enabling Duesenberg to bring four cars by boat to France. Experts wondered how the Duesenbergs, with their hydraulic brakes, would fare in a Grand Prix-type race. They seemed to get their answer early on, when Jimmy Murphy and Louis Inghibert both had braking problems and crashed. While Murphy nursed a cracked rib, his mechanic came up with the idea of reducing the size of the rear brakes, which kept locking up. He did it the old-fashioned way—with a hacksaw—and the two jumped back into their car and were on their way. This adjustment enabled the hydraulic brakes to work perfectly, allowing Murphy to wait until the last second before

HARRY MILLER

Like many others in the years prior to World War I, Harry Miller saw in auto racing a shot at fame and fortune. Rather than driving cars or building them, however, he focused on sparkplugs and carburetors. Miller reasoned that if he could make these items better than anyone else, all of the racers would buy them, and then every driver would want them. His first breakthrough came when he constructed a light-weight aluminum carburetor, and just as he planned, about three-quarters of the top drivers ordered them immediately.

But by the end of the war Miller had accumulated so much automotive knowledge that it seemed silly not to manufacture entire automobiles. He built beautiful, streamlined automobiles with light chassis and eight-cylinder double overhead camshaft engines—not for the public, but specifically for racing. These were the world's first single-seaters. If a driver just wanted the engine, that was fine. In 1922, Jimmy Murphy sent his Duesenberg to Miller and the result was the famous Murphy Special, which promptly smashed the 100-mph barrier at Indianapolis.

By 1923, Miller's 122 model was the talk of racing. It was designed with oval tracks in mind, and it dominated at Indy for years to come. From this success, he built cars for all manner of racing, and right through the 1920s, Millers won everything in sight. In 1925, Miller came out with a front-wheel-drive supercharged racer that blew everyone else off the track with its unprecedented cornering ability. Soon, no one but Duesenberg dared to challenge his supremacy in the building of race cars. In 1929, Miller appeared to be at the height of his powers. His cars finished first and second at Indy, and broke several speed records.

Harry Miller poses behind the wheel of a revolutionary four-wheel-drive racer he designed in 1932.

But the end was near. In the fall, the stock market crashed, draining millions from racing. Sponsorship money dried up quickly, as did the number of fans who paid their way into the big events. In 1930, the final blow to Miller came when AAA announced a new formula designed to lure the major auto manufacturers back into racing. The final nail in Miller's coffin was the rule stating that all cars had to be two-seaters, and that mechanics had to go back to riding with their drivers. Miller tried to retool, but could not remain profitable building "lesser" cars. By 1933, he was bankrupt. Miller's legacy continued for many decades. His foreman, Fred Offenhauser, bought the remnants of Miller's business and produced a new engine. The "Offy" engine became one of the classics in the sport. Miller died of cancer in 1943.

Jimmy Murphy (seated right, beside mechanic Ernie Olson) became the first American to win the French Grand Prix in his Duesenberg.

slowing down in the curves, and he surged into the lead. He crossed the finish line—his rib broken, his car suffering from a punctured radiator and a flat tire—to give an American automobile manufacturer its first victory in a major European race.

Back in America, Murphy won the 1924 AAA National Championship in the same car he drove to victory in France. He had purchased the Duesenberg after the Grand Prix, christened it the "Murphy Special," and then taken it to Harry Miller's Los Angeles factory, where it was fitted with a powerful new engine. The publicity generated by the Murphy Special made Miller America's engine guru.

In 1922, racing in Europe came all the way back, as Germany and Austria started competing again. Everyone was working on new ideas. The French and English were tinkering with engine design, while in Germany Mercedes began experimenting with supercharging. Count Sash Kolowrat, an Austrian film producer and driver, hired Ferdinand Porsche to build one of the small, highly efficient cars he had been pushing for since going to work at Austro-Daimler in 1909.

Italy had a major breakthrough in the French Grand Prix, although its victory was tinged with great sadness. The old warrior, Felice Nazzaro, rode to an impressive win in one of three newly designed Fiats entered in the race. Only after he crossed the finish line was he informed that a design flaw had caused the rear axle of his teammates' cars to snap. Pietro Bordino's accident took place as he slowed down for a curve, and he survived. Nazzaro's nephew, Biagio, was not as lucky. His axle gave out while he was accelerating on a straightaway, and he and his mechanic were killed when the car cartwheeled end-over-end at 100 mph. An examination of Nazzaro's winning car revealed that his axle was cracked in the very same place, and could have come apart at any second.

Italy was fast overtaking France as the dominant racing country in Europe. It had the fastest cars, the top drivers, and had found a way to make Grand Prix racing highly profitable, thanks to a course constructed on the grounds of the Monza Palace, which the King of Italy had turned over to the government when political reforms swept the country following World War I. Monza combined an oval track (like Indy) with a 6.2-mile circuit track—all of which could be viewed from a central grandstand location. This enabled the Milan auto club to charge admission to its events, which it channeled into enormous purses, and this attracted the top drivers and manufacturers in the world to Italy. Within three years the French followed suit, building "autodromes" outside of Paris and Marseilles. The first Italian Grand Prix held at Monza was won in 1922 by Pietro Bordino, who defeated Nazzaro to become the toast of Italian racing.

By the mid-1920s, it had become clear that manufacturers could no longer build one type of car and expect it to win road races and track races. With smaller and smaller engines capable of propelling vehicles at greater and greater speeds, focus began to shift to suspension and braking systems, transmissions, and especially to

improving how cars handle. It was at this point that the Europeans began concentrating on road racers. Engineer Vittorio Jano moved from Fiat to Alfa Romeo and was given a free hand to design supercharged vehicles. His P2s would soon prove to be the class of the circuit and bring Alfa the first manufacturer's World Championship in 1925. Meanwhile, Ferdinand Porsche joined Daimler in Stuttgart, Germany, and produced a car that gave Germany its first postwar win in a major race. The designs of Jano and Porsche would continue to influence racing for the next three decades.

American designers in the 1920s— Harry Miller in particular—were thinking about the demands of the oval track. His Miller 122s could be found in every major U.S. race, but he was determined to push the envelope. A car that could corner faster would have a big advantage in oval-track races, and that meant building a car low to the ground. The problem was that, with the engine in front and the wheels in the back pushing the car along, the prop shaft that connected them limited how low a driver could be situated in the car. To address this, Miller designed an automobile that used the front wheels to pull the car—what is now known as front-wheel drive. He also added a supercharged engine. The Indy 500 was won by Millers in 1926, 1928, and 1929. In 1927, there were 29 Millers entered at Indianapolis.

As the decade drew to a close, safety was becoming an issue on both sides of the Atlantic. The fame won by the era's best drivers was great for racing, but each time one met his doom it was cause for great sadness and concern. In one horrible year (spanning from 1924 to 1925), Jimmy Murphy, Joe Boyer, Dario Resta, and Antonio

Ascari—all ranking among the world's top 10 drivers—died in crashes. No one disputed that the blood-sport aspect of racing provided much of its mass appeal, but when drivers began dropping like flies, everyone agreed that engines had to be made smaller until the vehicles they powered could be made safer.

This rule had been used before with the idea of promoting safety, but as had happened in the past (and would happen again and again in the future) all it really did was provide an incentive for engineers to coax more power out of tinier motors. In Europe, the change came at a most inopportune time, as many manufacturers were short on cash. The prospect of having to retool factories to produce smaller, more powerful engines was not very appealing, so many car companies pulled out of racing and concentrated on competing in the showroom instead of on the track. At the same time, however, European racing fans demanded more action. Several new races were formed, including the British, German, Belgian, and Czechoslovakian Grand Prix, and there was a boom in "formula libre" events, which brought together all different sizes and types of cars on the same circuit. But with fewer companies making top-of-the-line racers, competition shifted from manufacturer vs. manufacturer to driver vs. driver. The remaining race-car producers still maintained their own teams, but they found a new profit center in selling vehicles to individuals entering races on their own.

In the United States, a similar situation was occurring. Besides pushing for smaller engines, the AAA addressed safety concerns by shutting down many of the nation's board tracks, which had caused more than

their fair share of fatal accidents. When the stock market crashed at the end of 1929, it set in motion a financial cataclysm that would greatly retard advances in American racing. For several years, in fact, the sport would lose momentum on both sides of the ocean.

The 1930s: Indy and Grand Prix Racing

The economic woes that overcame the world after the 1929 stock-market crash hit racing hard, but not everything went poorly at the track during the early 1930s. A lack of cash forced engineers to limit their focus to building more economic engines, so during this time no one was thinking too hard about building entirely new racing cars. In an attempt to lure U.S. manufacturers back into race-car production, the American Automobile Association introduced a "junk formula" that enabled modified stock cars to be competitive again. Whereas the Indianapolis 500 had been the exclusive domain of Millers and Duesenbergs in the late 1920s, in 1930 the event saw engines from Buick, Chrysler, Stutz, and Studebaker. By 1932, several companies had produced excellent racing versions of their touring cars, most notably Studebaker.

In Europe, Bugatti, Alfa Romeo, and Maserati dueled in most of the big races. Vittorio Jano designed the first competitive single-seaters for Alfa Romeo. They were light twin-engine cars with a prop shaft going from each engine to the corresponding rear wheel. A little slower in the straightaways, these "Monopostos," or P3s, could take corners without losing much speed and offered great traction. This design attracted the two top European drivers of the day,

FAST EDDIE

In 1910, a 19-year-old salesman for the Columbus Buggy Company decided a neat way to sell cars was to enter them in local races. After discovering he had a knack for pushing an automobile to its limits, he decided to quit selling and start driving full-time. The young man's name was Eddie Rickenbacker, and by the spring of 1911 he was good enough to finish 11th in the first Indianapolis 500. In 1913, he won $10,000 in a 100-mile event and used the money to put together his own racing team. By 1917, Rickenbacker was one of the most successful drivers and team owners in the country.

That year, however, he left the track and went into the service to become a flyer in World War I. Rickenbacker became America's most famous ace during the war, shooting down 26 German planes in seven months. After the war, he used his fame to raise money for the Rickenbacker Motor Company, but eventually it went bust. Never one to quit, Rickenbacker raised more money, and approached Indianapolis Motor Speedway owner Carl Fisher. Would he be interested in selling a piece of the track? The timing was perfect. Fisher, who knew he

Eddie Rickenbacker went from ace driver to World War I flying ace in a matter of months. A decade later, he purchased the Indianapolis Motor Speedway.

Rudolf Caracciola and Tazio Nuvolari. Nuvolari won the Italian Grand Prix in a P3 the first time the car hit the road in a major event. Incredibly, after the P3 won almost everything in sight during 1932, they nearly disappeared. Alfa Romeo decided to pull out of racing because it cost too much. The company gave the cars to Enzo Ferrari, who had been racing the company's old Monzas with his own team. For a time, this left Bugatti as Europe's only true factory-based racing team. Everyone else was modifying old Alfa Romeo Monzas or Maseratis. Racing looked like it was beginning to stagnate.

This situation changed dramatically in the mid-1930s, as two powerful influences converged simultaneously. In Europe and the United States, improvements in engine design had rendered the old safety-motivated size restrictions useless, so new limitations were placed on engines. The would have to invest a lot of money to modernize the facility, believed that buying Florida real estate was a wise investment. He sold the entire operation to Rickenbacker in 1927.

Rickenbacker's plan was to make "The Brickyard" the greatest track in the world by working with top auto manufacturers. He also believed that the top drivers should be promoted more aggressively. America was mad for sports during the 1920s, and yet there were relatively few homegrown racing heroes. Thanks to Rickenbacker's efforts, Wilbur Shaw and Louie Meyer—two of Indy's best—became well known throughout the country.

With famous drivers and well-known manufacturers racing at Indy, Rickenbacker then began to market the track itself, raking in millions in advertising and sponsorship deals. He then plowed this money back into the race, increasing the winner's purse and offering special bonuses. This further increased the prestige of Indy, which became important during the 1930s, as the Great Depression ravaged the U.S. economy.

After the 1933 race, Rickenbacker faced a tough decision. Five competitors died during the event, and there was a great outcry for better safety measures. With revenues dropping and no end to the Depression in sight, Rickenbacker swallowed hard and invested what little capital he had left. The brick surface was repaved with asphalt, retaining walls were strengthened, and a system of yellow and green lights was adopted to let the drivers know if there was trouble ahead. Other safety measures were taken. Restrictions on oil and fuel were passed to cut down on the deadly explosions that often accompanied serious crashes, and the field was reduced to 33 cars so everyone had more room to maneuver. And first-time drivers had to pass a special test before they were permitted to enter the race. These changes ushered in the modern era at the Indianapolis Motor Speedway.

Americans focused on fuel consumption, while the Europeans opted for keeping engine weight under 750 kilograms, or about 1,650 pounds. Meanwhile, in Germany, Adolf Hitler had come to power with a plan to rebuild his country's tattered reputation. One of the areas he chose was automotive design, and he set up a special fund to jump-start the German engineering effort. Hitler also offered large bonuses for car-builders who won Grand Prix races. Immediately, Ferdinand Porsche and the team at Mercedes began working on separate designs.

Each used lightweight alloy wheels and independent suspension to improve cornering and traction. Where their designs differed, however, was in the placement of the new lighter engine. Mercedes used a conventional eight-cylinder motor and placed it in the traditional place: the front end. Porsche, working with Auto Union, unveiled a design with the engine behind the

Tazio Nuvolari wins the 1938 British Grand Prix at Donington despite a painful injury to his ribs. In practice, he had crashed after hitting a deer.

driver. The cars were unveiled in 1934 and by mid-summer began winning everything.

So impressive were the German cars that Tazio Nuvolari—who had determined years earlier he could win more fame and money racing independently—grudgingly approached Auto Union for a job. He was rebuffed. The team already had Hans Stuck and Achille Varzi, and neither wanted to play second fiddle to Europe's top driver. Nuvolari did not even bother to go to Mercedes, which had the great Caracciola, as well as Luigi Fagioli and Manfred von Brauchitsch. Realizing he would not be able to compete against the Germans on his own, Nuvolari eventually went back to work for Enzo Ferrari at Alfa Romeo. There he got behind the wheel of the Bimotore, a car with two engines—one in the front and one in the rear—that also featured independent front suspension. It was a relatively crude answer to the sublime engineering of the Germans, but his skill as a driver eventually won out. Although Mercedes and Auto Union dominated again in 1935, it was Nuvolari in his Bimotore who stunned 300,000

fans at the fabulous Nurburgring to win the German Grand Prix.

The story continued over the next five years, with the German cars reaching speeds approaching 200 miles per hour and Nuvolari stealing an occasional race in an inferior Alfa Romeo. Auto Union developed a spectacular driver in Bernd Rosemeyer, who usurped the European Auto Drivers Championship from Caracciola in 1936.

Caracciola reclaimed his title in 1937, the same year Mercedes came out with a stunning new design called the W125. It looked like something out of the future, and it drove that way, too. Long, wide, and low to the ground, it was the most specialized racer ever built. It was assembled to go full-tilt for around 500 miles, and had to be taken back to the factory and completely overhauled after each race. In 1938, Auto Union suffered major setbacks when Rosemeyer was killed trying to set a speed record and Hitler asked Ferdinand Porsche to start work on his pet project, the Volkswagen. Nuvolari, who had been threatening to walk out on Alfa if it did not catch up to the Germans, did so in 1938 after his fuel tank split and he was badly burned during the season's first race. He went to work for Auto Union later in the season, restoring some of the company's pride with victories at the Italian Grand Prix and the Donington Grand Prix in England.

In 1939, with Germany and Italy allied against England and France, tension ran high all season long. The racing season ended in early September, after Germany invaded Poland. The final race before the start of World War II was the Yugoslav Grand Prix. Nuvolari won for Auto Union to put an exclamation point on a period marked by revolutionary German automotive design.

The Great Depression of the 1930s hit American racing hard. Harry Miller went bankrupt in 1932, even as his cars were winning races all over the country. Luckily, the pieces of his business were picked up by machinist Fred Offenhauser and draftsman Leo Goosen, and they produced a four-cylinder engine powerful enough to win the 1935 Indianapolis 500.

In 1937, with the economic crisis easing up somewhat, the decision was made to return the Indy 500 to its former status as the ultimate showcase for racing cars. The track was renovated, and limitations removed on supercharged engines as well as fuel consumption. In 1938, Europe and America both adopted a sliding scale that balanced out engine capacity and weight. This gave designers a lot of options, but it also meant that the top U.S. and European racing cars could appear on the same track for the first time since the 1920s. Wilbur Shaw won the race in a Maserati, and repeated in the same car a year later. Sadly, the onset of war put an end to what might have been a fascinating chapter in racing history, as England, France, and

Wilbur Shaw is greeted by a mob of radio and newspaper reporters after winning the 1939 Indy 500—his second victory at the "Brickyard." Shaw would later become president of the Indianapolis Motor Speedway.

IL MAESTRO

Every sport has its "iron man"—the athlete who defies the sands of time by performing at a high level long after his peers have left the sport. In auto racing, that person was Tazio Nuvolari. Between 1921 and 1950 he entered 145 races and won 70 of them. To survive 145 Grand Prix races is nothing short of miraculous, especially during the time when Nuvolari competed. To win nearly half of those events is still hard to comprehend.

The funny thing is that those who actually saw Nuvolari drive often worried that he would not survive the race. He was a ferocious competitor, unwilling to accept the fact that, for most of his career, he was driving inferior cars. He pushed his vehicle to its absolute limit and accepted nothing less than victory. Nuvolari had a special relationship with his cars, and seemed to know how to get the most out of each individual part. When he did not win it was usually because he crashed. Yet somehow, despite breaking every major bone in his body at least once—and being given his last rites on six separate occasions—Nuvolari continued to climb behind the wheel and win races.

Nuvolari got his first chance to drive during World War I, when he was assigned to the ambulance corps. After the armistice, his commanding officer took him aside and told him to look for some other kind of work—he was a menace. Undaunted, he got into motorcycle racing and became Italian champion within a few years. Nuvolari then devoted himself to automobiles.

Nuvolari lived for the turns. Though he weighed only 130 pounds and was not strong enough to steer the big, heavy racers of the day, he compensated by perfecting a method of fighting his way through turns. Nuvolari would go into a curve so fast that the wheels would lose traction with the surface. This made the wheel easier to turn. With the tail end spinning out and the nose pointing in, he then was in perfect position to blast out of the curve and up the next straightaway. It was a move few others dared to try, for when it did not work the car went flying off the track, often with deadly consequences. But Nuvolari, utterly fearless, took the turns faster and faster, and often came out of them screaming with delight or banging the side of his car in unbridled exhilaration.

His secret lay in his years as a motorcycle driver. Nuvolari claimed he could sense, within a pound, the maximum amount of weight each of his four wheels could take going through a curve. Without a doubt, the incredible balance he developed during his two-wheel days gave him an important edge.

The crowning moment of his career came in 1935, at the German Grand Prix. Going up against the cars built by Mercedes-Benz and Auto Union—some with the most powerful piston engines ever built—Nuvolari and his Alfa Romeo had no real chance for victory. The race was meant to be a showcase for Nazi Germany's automotive prowess. Entering a car that could not come within 20 mph of the top speed of the German vehicles, Nuvolari was an object of pity before the race began. Indeed, many of the 200,000 fans in attendance believed he should not sully his reputation as Il Maestro by entering such a pathetic little car. But Nurburgring was a strange course. It offered more twists, turns, and inclines than any other. His strategy was to let the fierce rivalry between Mercedes and Auto Union take its toll, and then move up among the screaming German cars and outduel the exhausted drivers through the curves. After grabbing the lead, a disastrous pit stop put him back to sixth. Nuvolari blasted out of the pits and began taking the curves even faster than usual. In no time, he had worked his way past the faster German cars and was back challenging for the lead. The Germans decided to ignore him—what Nuvolari was doing defied physics, and therefore he could not continue to do it. With Nuvolari on his tail, Manfred von Brauchitsch picked up the pace in an attempt to lose the pesky Italian. But try as he might, Nuvolari managed to stay close. When von Brauchitsch continued to push his car, his tires began to wear thin. Three laps from the finish, Nuvolari was only 32 seconds behind. The Mercedes crew could not chance a tire change, so they decided to let their driver go for broke. In the final lap, von Brauchitsch's tire blew and Nuvolari streaked by him for an unforgettable David-versus-Goliath victory.

Nuvolari competed until he was 58 years old, and continued to win right until the end. In his final race, at Mt. Pellegrino in 1950, he finished first in his class. That day he had to be lifted up out of his car, and he fainted while receiving his trophy. Nuvolari died three years later.

Germany halted racing altogether in 1940, with Italy following suit in 1941. Still, Americans carried forward many of the ideas pioneered by the Italians and Germans.

Drag Racing Takes Root

The years prior to America's entry into World War II saw the birth of a uniquely American form of racing. People in the United States had started to develop a love affair with the automobile during the 1920s, and nowhere was this more true than in California. In the late 1920s this region of the country was a much simpler place than it is today. The cities were still in their infancy, while the countryside was dominated by vast stretches of farmland dotted with the occasional sleepy town. Every so often, the quiet would be punctuated by the roar of a powerful engine.

Auto enthusiasts, especially young men in their teens, were becoming obsessed with

THE RACING WORLD AT WAR

Auto racing went on hiatus during World War II. Its manufacturers turned their efforts toward military production, while its top drivers, mechanics, and engineers were scattered across the world, at munitions factories and military bases, and on the front lines. Alfred Neubauer managed a repair shop for Luftwaffe and Wehrmacht vehicles. Ferdinand Porsche retooled his Volkswagen and came up with a military vehicle called the Kubelwagen. Enzo Ferrari's company stopped making cars and instead produced machine tools for the Italian military. In America, Eddie Rickenbacker worked for a time as the personal envoy for Secretary of War Henry Stimson. Rickenbacker's plane crashed in the Pacific and he survived for 24 days on a life raft before being rescued. Wilbur Shaw—winner of the Indy 500 in 1937, 1939, and 1940—worked in the aircraft division for Goodyear. In 1944, he was sent to the Speedway to test a new synthetic rubber for airplane tires. He found the Brickyard in shabby condition and contacted Rickenbacker, who mentioned that he might be persuaded to sell the track. Rickenbacker had diversified prior to the war, and had become a principal in Eastern Airlines. Shaw then contacted Indiana businessman Tony Hulman, who bought the track, plowed millions into upgrades and repair, and eventually made Shaw president.

speed. Perhaps because life moved at such a slow pace, these "hot-rodders" were consumed by the challenge of having the fastest car in town. They spent hours under the hood, trying to coax every last bit of power from their engines—tweaking a carburetor here, adjusting a cylinder head there. They were mechanical purists who took great pride in quality craftsmanship and attention to detail. To them, designing and building a powerful engine was as fulfilling as seeing it speed to victory. Late-night drag races were not only commonplace, they fulfilled an important function, giving young people something exciting to do and a place to congregate away from the prying eyes of their parents. Indeed, drag racing quickly developed its own culture. Caravans of racers and fans would set out at midnight for places like Muroc Dry Lake, located about 100 miles north of Los Angeles. If the car in front of you broke down, you stopped and helped repair the vehicle. Hot-rodders were a tight-knit group.

In drag racing's early days, drivers were allowed to build up a head of steam before being timed over a predetermined half-mile stretch. Using stripped-down, souped-up Model Ts, they achieved speeds in excess of 90 mph. Accurately determining a car's speed depended on a reliable timekeeper and timing mechanism. Hot-rodders experimented in these areas without much success until an enterprising watch specialist named

LIFE

COLLISION AND AIR SAFETY:
THE LESSONS OF GRAND CANYON
THE ZOOM IN DRAG RACING

STARTER FLAGS OFF
FORT WORTH DRAG RACER

20 CENTS
APRIL 29, 1957

As this 1957 LIFE magazine cover illustrates, drag racing grew from a cult sport to a national phenomenon within three decades.

J. Otto Crocker came along. He loved working with clocks, and his innovative ideas—such as a combination printer-timer that recorded times on a tape—helped advance the sport.

Slowly but surely, drag races progressed into organized events. Small entry fees were charged, and trophies were awarded to the winners. By the mid-1930s dozens of racing clubs had been formed, each seizing upon a colorful name. There were the Knight Riders, the Throttlers, the Idlers, and the Road Runners. Each claimed to have the best drivers, the craftiest mechanics, and the fastest cars.

At first, this took the form of good-natured boasting. But often this chest-thump-

ing led to violence. What should have been settled by the fastest cars increasingly came down to ugly brawls. When racers and their supporters gathered the night before big events, they circled their cars like wagons and slept inside for protection. In the late 1930s, local authorities got tired of breaking up fights and told the clubs that either they formalize their sport and make it safer, or the police would shut drag racing down. On November 29, 1937, five club leaders gathered for the first meeting of what was to become the Southern California Timing Association (SCTA). They discussed such things as providing ambulance service at events and dividing cars into classifications based on the engines they used. Other advancements soon followed. A technical committee was formed to inspect all cars before an event. The distance of heats was shortened. And most importantly, the size of the field in these heats was reduced to two cars.

After the formation of the SCTA, individual drivers and engineers began to make names for themselves. Stuart Hilborn developed a powerful fuel-injection system. He and his crew, always dressed in sparkling white uniforms, received their fair share of ribbing from competitors. But that stopped when their cars began approaching the 150-mph barrier. Vic Edelbrock, Sr. was one of the first in a long line of hot rodders who turned his love of drag racing into a successful business. Dissatisfied with the carburetion manifolds available, he began building his own. Soon Edelbrock was fielding hundreds of orders for his new device. Ultimately, he gave up racing and concentrated on his carburetor company.

As the drag-racing world entered the 1940s, it gained great credibility as its top drivers moved on to more mainstream racing. Manuel Ayulo and Jack McGrath—two of the biggest names of the day—each went from the dry lakes of California to the Brickyard of Indianapolis to compete in the Indy 500.

Bootleggers and the Birth of Stock-Car Racing

Stock-car racing also got its start in the United States during the pre–World War II era—and a very strange start it was. From 1920 to 1932, a federal law prohibited the manufacture and distribution of alcohol. The public's thirst for booze did not sub-

Bootlegging operations flourished during Prohibition. The "delivery men" for this illegal liquor became the pioneers of stock-car racing.

side, however, and this led to a booming industry in moonshine, a homemade corn liquor that packed a powerful punch. Moonshine was relatively simple to make, but smuggling it from a backwoods still to illegal speakeasies in towns and cities was not. Under the cover of darkness, bootleggers loaded their cars with illegal alcohol and sped across country loads to deliver their cargo. Following their every move were the cops—local, state, and even federal. Moonshining was a felony, and law-enforcement agencies did not hesitate to use deadly force. Given a choice between prison time, a shootout, or making a run for it, one can guess which option the moonshiners selected when they were caught. Needless to say, the faster they could move the better their chances for survival.

Over the years, bootleggers became pretty smart about their cars. They also shared tips on how to modify automobiles to perform and handle better than the vehicles chasing them. What they could not make themselves they often purchased through the mail. There is strong evidence to suggest that they were in communication with California hot-rodders, as well as engineers for some of the country's major automobile manufacturers. And thanks to some outrageous driving skills, the bootleggers were almost impossible to catch.

Even after Prohibition ended, moonshiners continued to operate. Their liquor was cheaper and stronger, and some actually claimed it tasted better than the store-bought stuff. So throughout the 1930s, the cat-and-mouse game between the bootleggers and the police continued, most notably in the Southeast. It was during this time that several drivers earned big reputations. Junior Johnson, who began hauling moonshine at the age of 13, was never caught once and became a legend by the time he was in his twenties. Fonty Flock actually looked for the police on his moonshine runs because he enjoyed being chased. The typical bootlegger loved to brag about his work behind the wheel and the power under his hood. When two of these fellows crossed paths it often led to a race.

As far as anyone can remember, the first such competition took place on a Sunday afternoon in a cow pasture in Stockbridge, Georgia, a few minutes from Atlanta. The event attracted a small crowd of curious onlookers. Everyone had a lot of liquor and a lot of fun, so it was agreed they would meet again the following week. This time a huge crowd showed up, and stock-car racing was born. From these humble beginnings it spread throughout the South.

The Postwar Years: Indy and Grand Prix Racing

Although auto racing went on worldwide hiatus during the war, advances in engineering continued unabated. As had been the case in World War I, many valuable lessons were learned from the aviation industry about the stresses high speed and maneuverability placed on engines and materials. Wartime research also produced such innovations as high-octane fuel, fuel injection, radial tires, and disk brakes.

As auto racing came back to life in the late 1940s, it hardly lacked enthusiastic supporters. What it needed, however, were functioning racing cars, rubber for tires, spare parts, and gasoline—all of which were in short supply. In Europe, a group of supercharged Alfa Romeo Alfetta 158s

dominated every race in which they were entered. The cars—designed by Gioachino Colombo—had been hidden in an Italian cheese factory during the war and emerged as the fastest surviving cars on the continent. Colombo and Enzo Ferrari hooked up briefly in 1945, after Ferrari left Alfa to set up his own company. Their collaboration led to the design of a new 12-cylinder engine, and Clemente Biondetti drove it to victory in Italy's prestigious Mille Miglia. Ferrari's success continued, as his cars won several major races in 1949, including the Italian Grand Prix, Swiss Grand Prix, and Czechoslovakian Grand Prix.

By 1950, European Grand Prix racing was back on its feet. The creation of the World Drivers Championship gave everyone something to shoot for, and new designs would soon challenge the remarkable Alfettas. Alfa Romeo would continue to dominate through 1951, however, thanks largely to the skills of veteran drivers Giuseppe Farina and Luigi Fagiola, British ace Reg Parnell, and racing's brightest new star, Juan Manuel Fangio. This group produced a winner in all 11 races Alfa entered in 1950, with

The 1938 "Alfetta" was so famous it even had its own trading card. The Tipo 158's dominance lasted for more than a decade.

MEANWHILE, DOWN IN FLORIDA...

Bill France, during his racing days. The reputation and experience he earned in the 1930s would serve him well after World War II.

In 1934, Bill France packed up his family and headed south from the Washington, D.C., area to Miami, Florida. They made it as far as Daytona Beach, where France set up shop as an auto mechanic. It seemed to be a fine place for such a business, even during the depths of the Depression. The city's flat, hard beaches were the perfect place to go after a land speed record, and for decades the fastest cars had roared down these beaches in thrilling time trials.

Soon after France arrived, however, Daytona began to fall upon hard times. Utah's Bonneville Salt Flats were less treacherous for high-speed driving than Daytona's beaches, and the speed kings were moving west. Daytona's city fathers, desperate to keep their city's racing heritage alive, approached France and local restaurant owner Charlie Reese in 1938 and asked the two to promote races. Their initial efforts met with success, and over the next few years Daytona Beach regained its place of prominence in the sport.

France had raced cars himself during the early 1930s, but became disillusioned by the unscrupulous people who promoted races. When he became a promoter, he vowed to clean up the sport in his small corner of the world. By 1941, Daytona became a favorite spot for drivers. They were treated well and got paid when they won. This simple idea would one day blossom into a multibillion-dollar industry, with Bill France at the helm.

Farina taking the first World Drivers Championship. In 1951, Ferrari and Alfa battled all season long, and came down to the final Grand Prix, in Barcelona, tied at three victories apiece. Fangio and Ferrari's top driver, Alberto Ascari, were also vying for the World Drivers Championship. Tire problems sank the Ferrari team, and Fangio cruised to victory in what would be the final Grand Prix appearance of the beloved but now-ancient Alfetta.

In the United States, all eyes turned to Indianapolis after the war. The Speedway had a new owner, local businessman Tony Hulman, and a new president, former driver Wilbur Shaw. The 1946 race featured prewar cars, and only nine managed to keep rolling through the finish. In 1947, Lou Moore—one of the most successful car owners of the prewar era—signed a deal with Blue Crown Spark Plugs and had Leo Goosen design two state-of-the-art front-wheel cars with Offenhauser engines. Driven by Mauri Rose and Bill Holland, the Blue Crown Specials blew away the field and battled right to the finish line, with Rose winning by 32 seconds. It was the same story the next two years, as Rose repeated in 1948 and Holland took the checkered flag in 1949. Finishing second to Holland (Rose had to drop out with mechanical problems) was Johnny Parsons, who was piloting a car designed by Frank

Kurtis. Kurtis was well known among drivers for his innovative dirt-track and Indy designs. During the 1950s, he would move to the forefront of the industry and, in fact, change the very look of the Indy 500.

Grand Prix Racing: The 1950s

The stranglehold of the Alfa Romeo Alfettas on Grand Prix racing ended after the 1951 season, but European automobile manufacturers had nothing to offer in the way of interesting replacements. The Ferrari 375 was the only thing close, and it did not have much competition in 1952. The problem was that a new formula for top-of-

THE ALFETTAS

When the Alfa Romeo Tipo 158 "Alfetta" was unveiled at Italy's Coppa Ciano in 1938, the little "voiturette" met with immediate success, placing first and second in the race. Generally, a great car design lasts a year or two before it becomes obsolete, but in the case of the Alfetta—which was designed by Gioachino Colombo after Vittorio Jano left Alfa—the story was quite different. When the war ended in Europe and racing resumed, everyone scrambled to see what had survived. Several Alfettas made it through the hostilities in pristine condition, thanks to some quick thinking. When the Nazis took over in Italy in 1943, the cars were hidden in a cheese factory and the Germans never discovered them. In order to bring the racing industry back at a slow, manageable pace, the new formula for postwar engines was set at a modest 4.5 liters, or 1.5 liters supercharged, which is what the Alfettas were.

So while designers tried to slap together new engines or modify old ones, the Alfettas—perhaps the greatest 1.5's ever built—had a huge advantage. This edge lasted into the 1951 season, when the last bit of power was squeezed from these engines and Alfa Romeo finally succumbed to hard-charging Ferrari. In the years prior to and following World War II, the Alfettas were literally in a class by themselves. The 13-year run of the Alfettas remains unprecedented in the history of motor sports.

Mauri Rose, winner of the 1947 Indy 500. His Blue Crown Special was the first great racing car of the postwar era.

the-line Grand Prix racers was going into effect in 1954, and most companies were focusing their efforts on that. So in 1952 and 1953, racing fans shifted their interest to a less powerful level of racing that had been introduced in 1948, "Formula B." As the top level of Grand Prix would come to be commonly called "Formula One," this second tier would be known as "Formula Two." A third, less-powerful classification, was "Formula Three."

Not surprisingly, almost all of the top drivers began competing in Formula Two races, including Fangio, who along with Argentine countryman Froilan Gonzales signed on with Maserati. Ferrari had an impressive stable of drivers, led by Ascari. The French and Germans had competitive cars and good drivers as well. But the really interesting development in Formula Two was the rise to power of the English, who

had been building Formula Three cars for several years, and had made great strides in Formula Two design. The key individuals in this subplot were owner Charles Cooper, whose liking for mid-engine vehicles would have a great effect on racing in the 1950s, and Stirling Moss, a young driver on the verge of greatness. At the 1953 Italian Grand Prix, Moss climbed into the seat of a T24 Cooper-Alta with fuel injection, disc brakes (the first time these had been used in a Grand Prix), and nitromethane fuel. Driving with intelligence and grit he finished fifth, but everyone at Monza knew that all that kept him out of the lead were some trifling mechanical problems.

The following season, Moss and the circuit's other stars got back into the Formula One business. The circuit attracted a few new names, as well as some familiar faces. As expected, Maserati and Ferrari entered awesome cars, but so did Lancia, which had been out of racing since the 1930s. The company was now owned by Gianni Lancia, whose father Vincenzo had been a pioneering driver at the turn of the century. Gianni hired the great Vittorio Jano to build his highly anticipated D-50, and signed Ascari, Eugenio Castellotti, and Luigi Villoresi to his driving team. Mercedes returned to Grand Prix racing with the sleek new W196 and hired a team of top drivers, including Fangio and prewar superstar Hermann Lang.

The first event of the 1954 season was the Argentinian Grand Prix. Racing had become a big deal in South America after the war. Fangio and Gonzales were already international superstars, and Argentina's dictator, Juan Peron, believed that staging a world-class race would greatly enhance his country's status abroad. Because the Mercedes W196 was not yet ready, Fangio was allowed to drive the new Maserati 250F, and he outdueled a trio of Ferraris to win. Still waiting for his Mercedes, he drove a Maserati in the Belgian Grand Prix and won there, too. Fangio got his W196 in time for the French Grand Prix, and he and fellow Mercedes driver Karl Kling put on a show, finishing 1-2 far ahead of everyone else. Fangio won again at the German Grand Prix and Italian Grand Prix to cap off a remarkable year for Mercedes and earn for himself a second World Championship.

Fangio was joined on the Mercedes team in 1955 by Moss, who had won his first Formula One event the previous year at Aintree. The beauty of the W196 was that it had been designed to perform in all types of races, with some basic modifications. Moss drove a streamlined 300SLR model to victory at the Mille Miglia, destroying the

Auto Racing

Juan Manuel Fangio

The great Juan Manuel Fangio. Fangio collectibles are still in high demand among collectors, more than four decades after his last race.

race's old speed record by 10 mph. He then won the British Grand Prix with teammates Fangio, Kling, and Piero Taruffi in hot pursuit. Fangio, who started the year by winning again in Argentina, won the Italian grand Prix, and Moss took the challenging Targa Florio.

On the surface, 1955 had been a wonderful year for Mercedes. Its cars had humbled Ferraris at nearly every stop, and fans marveled at the futuristic W196 and 300SLR. But behind the scenes there was trouble brewing. To stay competitive in the consumer market, the company needed to devote more of its research and development money to its regular cars. The feeling was that Mercedes would suffer in the racing world if it had to come up with new designs on a limited budget, so the decision was made to pull out of racing after 1955. If there was any chance the company might have stayed in the game, it disappeared at the 24-hour race at Le Mans. A 300SLR driven by Pierre Levegh smashed into the crowd at 150 mph, killing him and 83 spectators. The accident was not Levegh's fault, but it nevertheless gave auto racing—and Mercedes—a black eye. As a result of this tragedy, the sport was shut down in France, Switzerland, Spain, and Mexico, and the American Automobile Association withdrew from Fédération Internationale de l' Automobile (FIA), racing's international governing body.

In 1956, Fangio joined Ferrari and Moss went to Maserati. Ferrari had purchased Lancia after its top driver, Ascari, died in a freak crash, and began modifying the D-50. Maserati also coaxed better performance out of its 250F by lowering it by eight inches. Fangio and Moss dueled all year.

The 1955 crash at Le Mans shook the racing world on both sides of the Atlantic. Scores of spectators were killed.

Fangio won the Argentinian Grand Prix and British Grand Prix, while Moss rode to victory at Silverstone and captured the Monaco Grand Prix and Italian Grand Prix. An emerging star that year was Englishman Peter Collins, who won the Belgian Grand Prix and French Grand Prix as the number-two driver for Ferrari. In the Italian Grand Prix, he was running third when he saw his teammate Fangio pull into the pits with engine trouble. Had Collins kept going he probably would have won the World Championship. Instead, he gave his car to Fangio, who sped off after Moss. The 45-year-old Argentine star could not catch him, but he finished second, which gave him enough driving points to overtake Collins and win his fourth career World Championship.

The 1957 season saw Fangio move to Maserati, and he had another stellar campaign. The highlight of his year was a dramatic come-from-behind win at the German Grand Prix, during which he broke his own course lap record 10 times and slithered past Mike Hawthorn—Ferrari's rising star—and Collins, who thought they alone were dueling for the lead. That assured Fangio a record fifth World Championship. Not wishing to press his luck—and sensing the young British drivers and designers were about to overtake the Italians—he retired from racing the following summer.

Maserati saw this change coming, too. Although it continued to sell racing cars, it pulled its works team off the circuit in 1958, leaving Ferrari to represent Italy by itself. Meanwhile, Britain had four companies making Formula One cars: Vanwall, British Racing Motors, Cooper, and Lotus. Also, a Scottish millionaire named Rob Walker had put together his own racing team, which featured mid-engined Coopers. The Cooper

Fangio's fame helped establish Grand Prix racing as a truly global sport. Here a D-Type Jaguar streaks past cheering fans during the 1957 Cuban Grand Prix.

designs featured motors that were far less powerful than others on the Formula One circuit, but they were much lighter, which meant they could make up the time they lost on the straightaways by shooting nimbly through the turns.

In the first race of 1958, Moss drove Walker's car to victory at the Argentinian Grand Prix, marking the first time a World Championship race had been won by a mid-engined car, and the first to be won by a car entered by a team owner as opposed to a factory. Walker's car won again in Monaco, this time with Maurice Trintignant behind the wheel. Vanwall won both the Dutch Grand Prix and the Belgian Grand Prix. Ferrari regained some momentum with victories at the French Grand Prix and British Grand Prix, but lost its two best drivers—Luigi Musso and Peter Collins—in fatal crashes during the season.

As the decade closed, death also claimed Hawthorn, who had edged out Moss for the World Championship in 1958, and Tony Vandervell's ill health led to his pulling Vanwall out of racing. But British fortunes were still on the rise. Coopers now had full-sized Formula One engines, and driver Jack Brabham—who'd been Australia's top young racer in the postwar years—proved as valuable in the factory as he did behind the wheel. BRM had recruited a team of top drivers, while Lotus came out with the powerful new Mk-16. Aston Martin, a sports-car company that was regularly beating Ferrari in road races, decided to get into the Formula One business, too. And across England, there were more than 100 highly specialized manufacturers of auto parts who were all too happy to make something special for any one of these manufacturers. Stirling Moss, meanwhile, turned down several lucrative offers to drive for factory teams and chose instead to work for Rob Walker—a move that foreshadowed some interesting developments in the world of racing.

Indy-Car Racing: The 1950s

The fuel-injected Offenhauser engine continued to be the motor of choice at the Indianapolis 500 throughout the 1950s. The cars designed around it, however, went through quite an evolution. Johnny Parsons, runner-up in the 1949 500, finished first during the rain-soaked 1950 race. He was driving a car designed by Frank Kurtis with independent front suspension and a light triangular tubular frame, called the Wynne's Friction Special. In 1951 the race was won by Lee Wallard, who also drove one of Kurtis's fast, well-handling cars.

Kurtis made a major breakthrough in 1952, when he was approached by the Cummins company, which manufactured diesel-powered trucks. Cummins asked Kurtis to design an Indy car around its monster supercharged diesel engine. Kurtis came up with the nifty idea of turning the tall engine on its side, with most of its weight on the left side of the vehicle. This not only addressed the issue of aerodynamics, but because Indy only had left-hand turns this configuration actually helped the car go faster.

Whenever the Cummins Diesel Special cornered, its center of gravity shifted to the center of the car, meaning driver Fred Agabashian could keep up his speed without losing balance and spinning out. Kurtis designed a similar car for Fuel Injection Engineering, and with Bill Vukovich behind the wheel it nearly won. Critics, used to Indy's cigar-shaped racers, joked that Kurtis was polluting the Brickyard with the same "roadsters" the hot-rodders were driving. The following year, they came around to his way of thinking, as Vukovich drove a roadster to victory in the fastest, hottest, most grueling race anyone could remember. And by 1954—when he won again—the Roadster era of Indy racing was well under way.

In 1955, Kurtis improved on his early designs and came up with the KK500C. The crowd could hardly wait for the race to begin, as Vukovich and Jack McGrath (the fastest qualifier) would each be driving one of these cars. Through 57 laps the drama unfolded as advertised, but then something went terribly wrong. One car broke an axle and veered in front of another, which dropped down into the infield to avoid hitting it. When this car attempted to rejoin the race, it clipped another car, which tumbled in front of Vukovich. There was nothing he could do. Vukovich hit the car, flipped through the air and his car exploded into flames upon impact, killing him instantly.

Despite this tragedy, the race was another feather in the cap of Frank Kurtis, who watched as Bob Sweikert, in a KK500C, finished first. The following year nearly two dozen entries at Indy were roadsters. The race was won by Pat Flaherty, driving a roadster designed by A. J. Watson. This car had a left-mounted engine that stood straight up, putting even more weight on that side but creating a narrower front and thus less wind-resistance. In 1957, Sam Hanks won in a roadster featuring a newly designed Offenhauser engine that lay practically flat. The result was a lower, wider car with even more weight on the left. A smooth body with a rear tailfin for stability made the Belond AP Parts Special one of the most exotic ever to win the 500.

By 1958, everyone was monkeying around with Kurtis's original design, including Kurtis himself. One car had its oil tank outside the car, to shift even more weight to the left. But it was the Belond winning again, this time with Jimmy Bryan at the wheel.

Then, as quickly as the roadsters had appeared at Indy, they faded away. In 1959, the race was won by Rodger Ward in the Leader Card Special designed by A. J. Watson. Watson had been an opponent of the laydown design, and had spent several years perfecting an Indy car with an upright motor. He incorporated thinner aluminum and fiberglass into the body design, coaxed a little more power out of his engine, and installed a hydraulic jack system under the car, so that it could be lifted off the ground with compressed air instead of manual jacks. These improvements resulted in extra speed on the track and gained precious seconds in the pits. They also showed that the roadster design had been pushed to its limit, and could go no further.

NASCAR Racing: The 1950s

The economic boom in the United States that followed World War II put car ownership within the grasp of millions of people. The American romance with the automobile blossomed into a full-fledged love affair, and car manufacturers responded by giving consumers what they wanted: big, powerful machines. People not only liked to drive these monsters, they liked to watch them race. And as soon as the war ended, stock-car racing picked up right where it left off.

The first major race run in the U.S. after the war, in fact, was a stock-car competition at Daytona Beach in April 1946.

By this time, Bill France had gained considerable renown as a race promoter, and he moved to organize the sport before it fell into the wrong hands. Prior to the war, unscrupulous promoters had given stock-car racing a bad name. They would come to a town, rent a track, and spread word among local drivers and fans that a race would be run with a fantastic prize for the winner. The people and cars would come, admissions would be collected, and the promoter would be on his way out of town with the money before the race was over. As soon as racing restarted after the war, the same con men were at it again. France gathered together some of the biggest names in stock-car racing to discuss the formation of an official organization that would oversee the sport. So was born the National Association for Stock Car Auto Racing, or NASCAR. The organization would set rules to keep competition fair, provide insurance for drivers, and devise a point system to determine an annual champion. To distinguish NASCAR events from others being held in the South and Midwest—and to capitalize on the new-car craze—France suggested their races should only include cars fresh off the showroom floor.

The first official NASCAR race was run on February 15, 1948, in Daytona. France, who had been running races there for a decade, did everything—promoting the event, enforcing safety standards, even parking cars and dropping the starting flag. NASCAR required all entries to be new passenger cars, but allowed for alterations to each vehicle. This type of event was deemed "modified" stock-car racing. Soon after, other divisions were created, including the Grand National series for cars without any modifications. Red Byron, a driver and mechanic from Atlanta, won the inaugural NASCAR event at an average speed of more than 75 mph, but he wasn't the driver most fans buzzed about afterward. Joe Weatherly and Curtis Turner had thrilled the crowds in Daytona, speeding side by side down the straightaway section of track in the sand and then barreling into the following turn. Fans grew to love both racers for their competitive fire on the track and their colorful personalities off it.

Weatherly, known affectionately as Little Joe, was a real prankster, as well as the most superstitious driver on the circuit. Turner, an expert airplane pilot with a boundless sense of humor, fancied himself a "ladies' man." They were famous for throwing parties that lasted for days, and for playing practical jokes on each other and other unsuspecting targets. Turner's personal favorite was secretly turning off an engine of his private plane during a flight, and then turning to the poor guy in the passenger seat and asking him if he knew how to fly. Weatherly also was a pilot, though he never paid much attention to the instruments on the cockpit dashboard. More than once he took off destined for one location and wound up landing somewhere else hundreds of miles in the wrong direction. Weatherly and Turner drove in NASCAR events with the abandon they developed during their days as bootleggers.

The first event featuring exclusively new cars came in June 1949 at the Charlotte Speedway in North Carolina—an oval dirt track that measured less than a mile. After the race, the winner's car was inspected and found to be in violation of NASCAR rules.

Joe Weatherly (12) and Curtis Turner (26) duel at Daytona. Their combination of skill, daring and competitive spirit captivated fans in the early days of NASCAR.

Judges discovered that a wedge had been used to stiffen the rear springs, and driver Glenn Dunnaway was disqualified. Dunnaway was furious. He knew where the wedge had come from: Car owner Hubert Westmoreland had been using the vehicle for bootlegging all week and forgotten to remove the wedge before turning it over to Dunnaway for the race. Westmoreland took NASCAR to court, seeking his $2,000 first prize. During the trial, NASCAR attorneys repeated the word "bootlegger" over and over again, shaming Westmoreland and sending a clear message to others in his profession that the association wanted them out as car owners.

NASCAR grew quickly in power and influence, and drove unscrupulous promoters and bootlegging owners out of the business. Professional drivers, as they were now known, would for the most part only compete in races promoted by the organization. Racing fans, not wanting to waste money on events with lesser talent, followed the top racers to the various stops on the NASCAR circuit. Although the Daytona race would be run on sand for many more years, the dirt tracks that made up the NASCAR venues would begin to disappear. The first step in this process occurred in 1950, when construction was completed on the magnificent Darlington International Raceway in South Carolina. Darlington was the brainstorm of race promoter Harold Brasington. He had been to the Indianapolis Motor Speedway, and dreamed of building a similar track for stock cars. While most thought he was crazy, Brasington was willing to take the risk involved in financing his new facility. He was a smart man—in 1950, 25,000 people turned out for the first Southern 500. Even though Darlington was an immediate

success, however, the age of the paved speedway was still several years off. NASCAR still had some growing to do.

The man responsible for much of that growth was Carl Kiekhafer. He owned the Mercury Outboard motor company, and in 1955 decided to get into the stock-car racing business so he could learn more about engines. He hired Tim Flock and paid him the unheard of sum of $40,000 to be his driver, and he poured thousands of dollars into his car to ensure that it was in tip-top shape for every race. Flock won 18 Grand National races that year, encouraging Kiekhafer to form a "team" of racers for the 1956 season. Kiekhafer ran his like a company, and the results were fantastic. Flock, Buck Baker, Speedy Thompson, Herb Thomas, and Charlie Scott (the first African-American to compete at NASCAR's top level) won 34 races, including a record 16 in a row. But the paperwork and lifestyle changes Kiekhafer imposed on his maverick drivers made them miserable, and by season's end Flock and Thomas quit.

Disillusioned, Kiekhafer pulled out of racing after 1956, but his impact was lost on no one. The way to win was to build a team of drivers, and put a lot of money into your cars. Much of that money, however, would come back in the form of prizes and business generated by advertising. When Kiekhafer started in 1955, he had painted the words "Mercury Outboards" on the side of Flock's Chevrolet. Every time Flock won, Mercury sold more cars, and Chevrolet sales stayed the same. Kiekhafer changed the sign to read "Kiekhafer Outboards" and he began selling more of his boat engines. Clearly, fans read and reacted to advertising on winning cars.

Watching this episode carefully were

the major car manufacturers. They were encouraged by Kiekhafer's experiment, and felt that the headaches involved in controlling drivers were well worth the benefits to be derived from winning races. General Motors and Ford got into NASCAR in a major way, spending millions to put the best cars on the track and secure the top drivers. The circuit was buzzing as the 1957 season got under way. Never before had stock-car racing had so much money or prestige.

What no one counted on was the accident that occurred at Martinsville, Virginia. In a May event, a Mercury driven by Billy Myers collided with another car and went flying over the retaining wall. Among the spectators was an eight-year-old boy, who required brain surgery. As he clung to life, newspapers across the country gave daily front-page updates on his condition. The negative publicity got a lot of people fired at the car companies, and they pulled out of NASCAR as quickly as they had jumped in.

The circuit limped along for the rest of 1957 and all of 1958, with the drivers working pretty much for themselves. Fortunately, the bad luck of 1957 had not kept fans away, so there was plenty of money to keep NASCAR moving along. Still, Bill France knew that he had to keep stock-car racing moving forward. The sport needed a big event, and he knew exactly where it should be: right in his own back yard—Daytona.

France had been trying to gain approval for a major venue in Daytona for nearly a decade, but local politicians balked at the idea. What was wrong, they wondered, with the existing course? France's answer was that on a flat track, cars could only pass on the straightaways. A speedway like Darlington, with high banked turns, would enable them to pass on the curves. This, he

claimed, was one of the most exciting aspects of Indy-car racing. For stock cars, though, the turns would have to be even higher and broader because the vehicles were heavier and wider than Indy cars. Eventually, France convinced the city to lease him the land. He then sold 300,000 shares of stock for a dollar each, and borrowed another $600,000 from oil baron Clint Murchison. France also pre-sold thousands of tickets for the first race, and sank that money into construction, too.

When Daytona International Speedway was done, it left everyone in awe. It was two-and-a-half-miles around, with the kind of high-banked turns and long straightaways that would enable divers to increase their speed by more than 25 mph. The days of dirt-track driving were numbered. NASCAR was about to go big-time.

Drag Racing 1946–1960: "Shot Rodders" and the NHRA

America's hunger for new cars in the years following World War II had an interesting effect on drag racing. Whereas the hot-rodders of the 1930s had to scrounge for cars and parts, there were now mountains of raw material for the sport's enthusiasts. The timing could not have been better, for drag racing gained thousands of converts after the war. These newcomers, however, were different than their fathers, uncles, older brothers, and cousins. They were less interested in the inner workings of an engine and more concerned with the end result: speed. Also, they were not children of the Depression, and therefore they did not always value concepts such as simplicity and economy.

A 1950s picture postcard from Daytona Beach shows the old sand straightaway with waves crashing in the background. A few years later, a modern "Super Speedway" would take its place.

Many of the new drag racers had deep pockets and did not hesitate to spend their money. They eagerly bought up the classic used cars on the market, and then transformed them into glamorous high-performance hot rods. Those who were short on cash sometimes stole what they could not buy, bringing to the sport an unsavory element. They went on midnight "auto supply runs" to steal parts for their cars. So proficient did they become at stripping autos, one could be dismantled in a matter of minutes.

The new hot-rodders raced anywhere there was an open stretch of road—even if it happened to be a town's Main Street. Drag-racing purists looked down on their younger brethren. They called them "shot rodders" because of their irresponsible and law-breaking driving habits. They were viewed as vandals with disrespect for just about everything. The sport had worked extremely hard to legitimize itself in the eyes of law-enforcement officials and regular townspeople prior to the war. Now in the late 1940s hot-rodding found itself near the brink of extinction. The sport needed decisive action if it was to survive. More accessible racing venues were needed, as well as tighter restrictions on drivers and fans. By this time the dry lake beds could no longer accommodate the huge throngs that attended hot-rod events, nor the piles of garbage they left behind.

The problem of where to hold these meets was solved fairly easily. During the war, a lot of air bases had been constructed, especially in coastal states such as Califor-

GOOD OL' BOYS

The drivers who built the popularity of NASCAR in the 1950s were a wild bunch. In the years that have passed, many have achieved folk-hero status, while others (usually the tamer ones) have faded into obscurity. The names that dominated stock-car racing in its early years were Herb Thomas, Lee Petty, Buck Baker, and the Flock brothers.

Thomas was ranked among the top five drivers every year from 1951 to 1956. In his first four seasons as a regular driver he amassed 39 victories. He had lived a hard life before he came to NASCAR, working like a dog every day since the age of 10 and having nothing to show for it except the face of a man twice his age. Thomas had a backwoods drawl, and was not particularly quick-witted, but once he got behind the wheel, he was simply brilliant. Somewhere in that head of his a racing computer clicked away, and he was as measured and calculating a driver as there was on the circuit.

Buck Baker, one of NASCAR's biggest stars during the 1950s. He won 24 races in 1956 and 1957.

Petty came to the NASCAR circuit after a career as a truck driver, mechanic, and illegal drag-racing champion. His two sons, Richard and Maurice, worked as his pit crew. Their teamwork and hands-on knowledge of stock-car engineering enabled the Pettys to keep Lee's car on the road, and give him an extra edge when he needed it. He taught his boys that second place did not exist—you either won or you lost. Throughout the 1950s, Petty never ranked lower than fourth in the point standings, and won a total of 54 races between 1949 and 1961. His last big race was the 1961 Daytona 500. Petty's car hopped the fence and he suffered internal injuries and a badly broken leg. This effectively ended his racing career, but signaled the beginning of Petty Enterprises, starring Lee Petty's son Richard, and later his grandson Kyle.

Thomas and Petty were very good drivers, but not great ones. They survived races as much as they won them. Buck Baker, on the other hand, was an immense talent. In 1956 and 1957, he entered 88 races and finished first or second 38 times.

Off the track, he was a party animal. Baker was a big drinker and a big fighter—every bit the stereotype of a 1950s driver, and then some.

The Flocks were also talented, particularly Tim. He won an amazing 18 races in 1955, and captured 8 in 1951, when he won his first season championship. Fonty, who was three years older, finished second to Tim in 1951 and won a total of 19 races in his career. After walking away from a gruesome wreck at Daytona in 1957, he quit racing. The eldest brother, Bob, had less success than his two siblings. He entered just 36 races in his career, winning 4. The Flocks loved the pre-race atmosphere, often coming into a town several days before an event to promote it for little more than meal money. All three brothers came from a bootlegging family, and got interested in stock-car racing when they found local law enforcement could not keep up with them. As Fonty liked to say, "We could send to California to get special parts to modify our cars . . . the sheriff couldn't afford to do that."

nia. Most of these facilities were either shut down or rarely used after 1945. The SCTA and other hot-rod organizations began holding events on these long, smooth, abandoned tarmacs, which were ideal for drag racing. In 1950, the California Highway Patrol gave its official blessing to a big meet at an abandoned Navy airship base, signaling a major step in drag racing's march toward legitimacy.

In 1951, the need for tighter regulations was addressed when the National Hot Rod Association (NHRA) was formed. With a governing body to set policy, the sport had a way to police itself. The NHRA concentrated a good deal of its efforts on making the sport safer, requiring protective devices such as roll bars and scattershields for all cars, and crash helmets for all drivers. The NHRA also helped spread the gospel of hot-rodding, embarking on national tours during which the association's leaders preached to audiences about the wonders of drag racing and demonstrated the awesome

power of their cars. To its astonishment, the NHRA discovered that a great appreciation for the sport already existed in many corners of the country. In fact, dragsters in Colorado, Kansas, Pennsylvania, and Florida had already begun to organize themselves. One of the drivers getting his start at this time was Don Garlits, a native of the Sunshine State, who loved everything about racing—from working on cars to driving them at top speeds. In the years to come he would establish himself as the undisputed king of the drag strip. Thanks to the SCTA and NHRA, drag racing cleaned up its image. These associations made it clear to its members that there was no room in their sport for hoodlums and delinquents. They accomplished this not just through public-relations tours, but through tight rules and regulations. By the mid 1950s, there was no way an "outlaw" could survive on the circuit; everyone had to play by the rules.

Those rules were relatively simple. Cars were separated by category. For instance,

THE HUDSON HORNET

The legendary Hudson Hornet, with Marshall Teague behind the wheel. He driove his Hornet to victory 7 times in 1951 and 1952.

Of all the makes entered in NASCAR events during the early 1950s, the biggest and clunkiest had to be the Hudson Hornet. Compared to the Cadillacs, Chryslers, Fords, Lincolns, Nashes, Oldsmobiles, and Plymouths on the circuit, Hudsons looked downright primitive.

But in 1952, Hudsons won 40 of the 48 events they entered—a staggering achievement, considering their engines were practically obsolete. Hudson—a minor company compared to the "big three" manufacturers, GM, Ford, and Chrysler—understood what it took to win stock-car races. The company's engineers worked closely with NASCAR drivers and mechanics, listening to their problems and addressing their needs. They devised ways to improve handling and safety, and explained how to get the optimum amount of power from Hudson engines. At a time when the sport was beginning to take off, Hudson's name was the one most closely associated with stock-car racing, and this drove its competitors crazy. By 1953, American auto manufacturers began paying close attention to NASCAR, and started working more closely with its key people. Although it would be a few more years before the first big sponsorship deals, the die was cast—all thanks to the lowly Hudson.

hot rods always raced hot rods, and stock cars always raced stock cars. The field would stage one-on-one, single-elimination heats until one driver, known as the "Top Eliminator," was left. The distance of each race was fixed at a quarter-mile. Fans loved this setup because it was simple and understandable. If you won, you got to race again. If you lost, you were done for the day.

Once drag racing had cleaned up its reputation, the stage was set for fantastic breakthroughs in car design and performance. At the beginning of the 1950s hot rods were moving at speeds slightly faster than 100 mph. Within a few years, drivers regularly topped the 150 mark. The improvements that made these speeds possible came from everywhere—from individual owners tinkering in their garages to major manufacturers like General Motors, which assigned some of its brightest people to engine-building projects.

It was a fun time to be involved with the sport. On any given weekend, a fan was likely to see something totally new. Racers tried anything during this period. Some built cars with more than one engine. Others, like Art Arfons and Bob Tennant, used airplane engines in their dragsters, which they dubbed the "Green Monster" and the "Little Monster," respectively. A few drivers began using different types of fuel, opting for more powerful alternatives to regular pump gasoline. Speed records began to fall with astonishing regularity. Body-design techniques were also advancing. Hot-rodders searched for ways to make their cars lighter, so they eliminated anything that added weight, including the transmission. They focused on minimizing wheel spin, developing wider tires with gummy surfaces. And they transferred more power to the ground by lowering a car's center of gravity.

Fans loved the heart-pounding action produced by dragsters. The roaring engines and awesome spectacle of these machines were worth the price of admission several times over. And if a record happened to be set—a distinct possibility at any NHRA meet during the mid-1950s—well, that was considered a bonus. Drag-racing fans liked the idea that they supported the fastest cars in the world, and in 1955 their sport moved from its regional beginnings and began to perform on a bigger stage. The first NHRA National Championships were held that fall in Great Bend, Kansas. This marked the first of the big annual meets. Many more would follow, especially as rival organizations like the American Hot Rod Association formed and scheduled its own events.

At these early races, dragsters from California had the upper hand. They had always walked with a confident stride, proudly proclaiming they were responsible for the birth of the sport. Now, as if to remind the world of their rightful status as hot-rod royalty, their names dominated the record books. But in 1957, the winds of change started to blow from the east, where a young man

Art Arfons's "Green Monster"—part dragster and part jet plane

named Don Garlits reached a record speed of 156.5 mph at a meet in Florida. A week later, he bettered that mark. West-Coast drivers did not like being upstaged by this eastern hotshot. The East-West rivalry that developed proved extremely beneficial to the sport. It gave drag racing a truly national scope, and spurred improvements that would see dragsters approach 200 mph by the end of the decade.

Grand Prix Racing: The 1960s

The racing world had barely blinked when Stirling Moss drove Rob Walker's Cooper T45 to victory at the Argentinian Grand Prix back in 1958. The idea that an entrepreneur's car could outdo a factory car seemed absurd, and the Moss victory was dismissed as a mere aberration. But it was not. In fact, a revolution took place in Grand Prix racing during the 1960s, as more garage owners like Walker began getting into the sport—and winning.

As the automotive industry became more sophisticated, these men actually had an advantage over automobile manufacturers in that they could build a car "cafeteria-style," picking the best components from various suppliers and assembling a superior racing car. If a part did not work, they tossed it in the trash, made a few phone calls, and got what they needed. When a factory faced the same problem, they had to send their designers back to the drawing board, losing precious time and money.

Although this was a new phenomenon in Europe, it had long been the case on the other side of the Atlantic. In the United States, this approach to car-building had been standard operating procedure since before World War

II. In Europe, the shift toward entrepreneurial ownership began in earnest in 1960, when Walker took a liking to the lightweight Lotus 18. In anticipation of the new Formula One specifications for 1961 (which would require lighter cars and smaller engines) he moved Moss from the Cooper to the Lotus, and the British star immediately drove it to victory at the Monaco Grand Prix.

With the new Formula One specifications in 1961, the racing world wondered if the mid-engined British cars could hold the advantage they had gained during the late 1950s. The Brits had lobbied against the new formula, while Ferrari had accepted it and spent more than a year designing its 156 "Sharknose" car. Ferrari had also assembled a crack team of drivers, including Wolfgang von Trips and Americans Phil Hill and Richie Ginther. Naturally, fans of Ferrari were expecting big things.

American Grand Prix star Phil Hill celebrates his victory in the 1961 Italian Grand Prix.

Moss won the year's first event at Monaco in a Lotus 18, but after that it was all Ferrari. Von Trips won the Dutch Grand Prix, Phil Hill won the Belgian Grand Prix, and Giancarlo Baghetti—driving a Ferrari for an independent team—took the French Grand Prix. But a year that had begun with such promise ended in disaster. At the Italian Grand Prix, von Trips collided with Jim Clark's Lotus and his Ferrari ripped through the crowd. Fourteen spectators died, as did von Trips. Hill won the race for Ferrari and took the World Championship, but Enzo Ferrari decided to shut down the team for the rest of the year. To make matters worse, at season's end, Ferrari's chief engineer and team manager both left the company.

That left the door open for new challengers. The move toward entrepreneurial team ownership continued, especially in England, with the emergence of the Lola garage sponsored by Bowmaker, and Motor Racing Developments, which was founded by Australian driver Jack Brabham and designer Ron Tauranac. Meanwhile, Colin Chapman of Lotus supplied new 24s to Brabham and another privately owned British team. For his own drivers—Jim Clark and Trevor Taylor—Chapman produced the Lotus 25, the first car built with a "monocoque" chassis. This idea was first used in aircraft design during World War II, and basically it meant constructing an outer shell that would support itself and thus reduce a vehicle's weight by removing its heavy framework.

The Lotus 25 was just one of several new cars hitting the scene. BRM came out with its 578, which Graham Hill drove to victory in three minor races early in 1962. Cooper came out with the T66, which featured a tubular space-frame. Porsche, which had reentered Formula One racing in 1961,

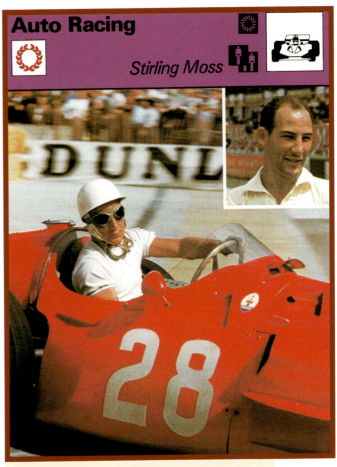

Auto Racing

Stirling Moss

British legend Stirling Moss, for whom a top-notch ride was rarely "in the cards." He finished his career with 16 Grand Prix victories.

created the 804 with an air-cooled engine that used carburetors instead of fuel injection. The company hired American Dan Gurney to drive.

Graham Hill, driving for BRM, won the first big race of the 1962 season, the Dutch Grand Prix. English dominance continued, with Bruce McLaren taking the checkered flag at Monaco in a Cooper T66, and Clark winning in Belgium in the new Lotus 25. The season came down to a battle between Graham Hill and Jim Clark, with Clark taking the World Championship with a

Jim Clark speeds to victory at the 1965 Indy 500. He won five Grand Prixes in a row later in the season, and was a top driver until his tragic death in 1968.

come-from-behind victory in the South African Grand Prix, the season's final race.

Clark's title was not a fluke. The following year also belonged to the 26-year-old British star. In fact, his only losses in Grand Prix events were the result of car trouble. At one point Clark guided his Lotus to victories in Holland, Belgium, France, and England to become just the third Grand Prix driver to win four consecutive races. A win at the Italian Grand Prix clinched the World Championship, and he won the Mexican Grand Prix to finish out the season and establish himself as the most gifted driver since Fangio.

The first half of the 1960s had belonged to British cars and drivers, with Lotus and Jim Clark leading the way. But with Coventry-Climax bailing out of the racing busi-

ness, the British teams were caught without a reliable supplier of engines. Each attempted to modify existing engines, knowing full well that its European competitors had been working on the new formula motors for a year or more. Also, the Cooper factory had been purchased by the Chipstead Motor Group, which had ties to Maserati, and Lola was now working with U.S. engine-builder Ford.

The first race of the 1966 season nevertheless went to a British driver, Stewart, who maneuvered a BRM with a bored-out Climax engine past the favored Ferraris to win at Monaco. Brabham won the French Grand Prix—making him the first driver to win a Grand Prix in a car he designed, built, and owned. He then went on to win the next three major events and earned his third World Championship. Brabham unveiled a new car in 1967 that was designed to take full advantage of the new Formula One rules. It was called the BT24, and it won its first race, the Monaco Grand Prix, with Denny Hulme at the controls. Another debut winner in 1967 was the Lotus 49, which had a completely redesigned Cosworth DFV engine that was mounted behind the driver.

British racing had more than held its own, and the talk of the sport was the new Cosworth engine, which embodied the kind of partnerships that were becoming increasingly common at the top levels of auto racing. Colin Chapman of Lotus had convinced Ford to put up the cash needed for his friends Mike Costin and Keith Duckworth (hence the company name Cosworth) to produce an eight-cylinder motor. They struck upon the idea of combining two of the company's highly regarded four-cylinder, four-valve models and coming up with a "double four-valve," or DFV model.

After Clark won the 1967 Dutch Grand Prix, cars with the DFV engine took the next 11 Grand Prix pole positions. It was quite obvious that this was the engine that would dominate Formula One, and it was almost universally adopted by the end of the 1960s. With a "standard" engine, the focus of the sport's top minds shifted toward improving their cars in other ways. It touched off a remarkable evolution in race car technology, starting with the extensive use of front and rear air foils (or "wings" as they were called) and moving in virtually every direction during the 1970s.

The 1960s closed on a couple of sad notes. After surpassing Fangio with his 25th Grand Prix victory in 1968, Jim Clark skidded off the course and into a wooded area

Scotland's Jackie Stewart, a great star and advocate for driver safety

during a Formula Two race in West Germany. There were no spectators nearby, and no other drivers were near him when the mishap occurred. By the time he was found and rushed to the hospital, it was too late. Clark died from his injuries. Another tragedy followed soon after, when a promising young driver named Jo Schlesser crashed and was roasted alive in a pool of burning gasoline at the French Grand Prix. The race marked his debut on the circuit, as well as the unveiling of the much-anticipated Honda RA302. As a result of these tragedies, the drivers—led by the increasingly influential and vocal Jackie Stewart—demanded and won key improvements in safety, including onboard fire extinguishers and better emergency care at races.

Indy-Car Racing 1960–66: The British Invasion

The Indianapolis 500 celebrated its 50th anniversary in 1961, and a capacity crowd was treated to a dizzyingly fast race. It came down to a two-man duel between veteran Eddie Sachs and 26-year-old A. J. Foyt. In a thrilling finish, he edged Sachs by less than nine seconds to win his first of four Indy titles. The 1962 race was won by Rodger Ward, marking the 16th year in a row the Indy victor had an Offenhauser engine.

Present at the race was Colin Chapman of Lotus, who had been invited by his friend, driver Dan Gurney. Chapman sensed a marvelous opportunity. In his opinion, Indy car technology had fallen far behind that of Grand Prix racers. Yet here was the winner of the 500 collecting a $125,000 grand prize—several times larger than the first-place money at the richest Grand Prix. Chapman decided to devote himself to building an Indy winner. He knew Ford was anxious to unseat Offenhauser as Indy's engine of choice, and that the company had already approached team owner A. J. Watson,

whose cars had won the last four Indianapolis 500s. Ford had gotten nowhere with Watson, and talks with other American designers did not seem to be bearing any fruit. Would Ford talk to a British designer? Chapman believed they would.

So after Jim Clark won the 1962 U.S. Grand Prix in a Lotus, Chapman took a chance and approached Ford. He found the people in Detroit were just as anxious to take on Indianapolis as he was, and they made a deal to build a Lotus with a powerful, lightweight Ford engine. In 1963, Chapman entered two cars at Indy, driven by Clark and Gurney. There were initial snickers when the tiny Lotuses showed up, but when they hit speeds of 150 mph in qualifying there were a lot of worried faces along pit row. The lighter cars were not only fast, but theoretically they could complete the race with only two refueling stops—one less than the American cars.

A. J. Foyt, age 26, celebrates his first Indy 500 win. He would win three more times.

Only a weird set of conditions denied Chapman's cars a victory. Parnelli Jones built a small lead over Clark, suggesting that the race would come down to that extra pit stop. Jones smartly made his extra stop while a yellow caution flag was out and rejoined the race with a five-second lead. But his car was leaking oil. This caused several spin outs, which kept the race under caution until there were only seven laps to go. By then, it was too late for Clark to pass Jones, and he finished second. Chapman was among those who were quite vocal about the unfairness of allowing Jones to race with a leaky engine. Eddie Sachs, who spun out twice on Jones's oil, gave him a piece of his mind at the victory luncheon. Jones responded with a knuckle sandwich.

Undaunted, Clark returned to Indianapolis in 1964. He found that he had made quite an impression. All of the roadsters entered had been reconstructed so that they would be light enough to complete the race with just two pit stops. And seven cars—including his Lotus—had the new Ford engine. A terrible crash on the second lap took the lives of Sachs and rookie Dave MacDonald, as their fully fueled cars exploded into flames. When the race resumed, the Lotuses went out, Gurney's with a mechanical problem and Clark with a collapsed wheel. Foyt and Jones competed for the lead until Jones's car caught fire after a pit stop, and only five cars managed to finish the race. Foyt won in an Offenhauser-powered car designed by A. J. Watson.

Foyt's victory marked yet another high point in the Texan's career, but it was also the last time a front-engined design would win the Indy 500. In 1965, Chapman finally broke through. Clark won the race in a Ford-powered Lotus and became the first European driver to take the checkered flag at Indy in nearly 50 years. More than half of the cars starting in 1965 had Ford engines. By 1966, only one front-engine car qualified for the race.

The start of the 1966 Indianapolis 500 featured two soon-to-be-familiar sights in the front row: Mario Andretti in the pole position, and the blazing red logo of Scientifically Treated Petroleum (STP), which agreed to sponsor Clark's Lotus. Meanwhile, Dan Gurney was at the race, but not as a Lotus driver. He had formed Eagle Racing, which designed cars for Indy and Formula One. He was seated in a car of his own design, in the seventh row. Other drivers familiar to Formula One aficionados were Graham Hill and Jackie Stewart, driving Lola-designed cars. The Lola team, backed by Englishman John Mecom, wanted a crack at the first prize after Clark brought home a $166,000 winner's check the year before. It was nothing short of a British invasion. Hill won the race, edging Clark in a disputed finish. The American racing establishment watched helplessly as the first- and second-place checks headed back to Britain.

Indy-Car Racing 1967–69: Americans Take Back the Brickyard

The British dominance at Indy would be short-lived, as U.S. designers came up with a dozen different ways to beat the British by the end of the decade. The most interesting originated from the fertile mind of STP owner Andy Granatelli, who had been entering cars at Indy for two decades. To stem the tide of foreign competition he hired Ken

Wallis to construct an Indy car around a Pratt & Whitney jet helicopter engine, and talked Parnelli Jones into driving it in the 1967 race. Called the "Whooshmobile" by the racing press, the car literally rocketed into the lead and was on its way to victory when, with just three laps to go, a bearing failed and Jones had to pull out of the race. A. J. Foyt—driving a Ford-powered Coyote engine—steered clear of trouble to win his third Indy, two laps ahead of second-place finisher Bobby Unser. Chapman's Lotuses, driven by Clark and Hill again, were barely a factor.

A Ford engine had won Indy again, but the folks at Offenhauser had not given up. In an attempt to regain their dominant position at Indy, Leo Goosen and his design team came up with a light and powerful turbocharged four-cylinder engine. Turbocharging had been used in airplanes and trucks for years, but this was the first time it appeared in a racing engine. In 1968, Bobby Unser won with an "Offy" engine, but not without a scare from Lotus, which sent three jet-powered cars to Indy under the direction of Granatelli. After the race, these engines—considered to be too dangerous—were outlawed. The decade closed out on a couple of interesting notes: Ford joined Offenhauser in the production of turbocharged engines, and Andy Granatelli finally got his first Indy winner when Andretti outlasted Foyt in the 1969 race.

NASCAR Racing 1960s: Hitting the Big Time

The 1960s saw stock cars first challenge and then actually surpass Indy cars as America's most popular form of auto racing. Following

on the heels of Daytona were new superspeedways in Atlanta and in Charlotte, North Carolina. Darlington was thriving, too, drawing 50,000 fans to the Southern 500 in 1960. With four superspeedways, NASCAR was able to generate unprecedented interest in its Grand National series, and this convinced corporate sponsors to consider reestablishing ties with the sport. They were impressed that, in little more than a decade, stock-car racing had captivated the public's imagination, especially in the South and Midwest. The spectacle of drivers bunched a few inches apart at speeds approaching 150 mph—in the same cars millions of Americans had in their driveways!—was absolutely mesmerizing.

The sport's amazing growth during the 1960s was not due to marvelous technical innovation—there were two basic engines being used, and body design was pretty much dictated by whatever consumers were buying in the showrooms. What drew the fans in droves were the drivers, who were more like the fans than athletes in any other major sport. They were also far more accessible than other sports stars. Imagine baseball fans being able to stroll around the field during warm-ups and chat with their favorite players. That was basically the setup at most stock-car events. This connection attracted hundreds of thousands of fans, and ultimately fueled NASCAR as it steadily moved from dirt tracks to superspeedways.

As the 1960s began, fans had a group of veteran stars to root for, including Joe Weatherly, Fireball Roberts, Rex White, Junior Johnson, Jack Smith, and Lee Petty—all of whom started during the sport's bootlegging days. Among the notable newcomers were Ned Jarrett, David Pearson, and Richard Petty. Jarrett had been racing since the early 1950s, although he started under an assumed name, fearing that his parents might find out. Like so many NASCAR champions, he came up through the ranks, winning enough second-tier races in 1957 and 1958 to earn a shot at the Grand National series. Good showings in 1959 and 1960 got him a sponsorship deal and a better car, and in 1961 he earned enough points to become Grand National champion. A dirt-track specialist, he won a total of 50 NASCAR races during his career, including 15 in 1964 and 13 in 1965, when he took his second Grand National title. Jarrett retired at age 34—an age when many drivers typically enter their prime—to become a race promoter, and later a television commentator.

Pearson made his debut in 1960 and went on to win an incredible 105 races. In an era when most NASCAR races were still run on small ovals, Pearson possessed a complete package of driving skills. He won on dirt, he won on asphalt, he won long races, and he won short ones. Like Jarrett, he worked his way up the auto-racing ladder, showing great promise but failing to attract a sponsor. In 1960 he bought his own car and did well enough to get backing for the 1961 season. That year he became the first driver to score victories on three of NASCAR's four superspeedways. After some up-and-down seasons in the mid-1960s, Pearson closed out the decade with three Grand National titles in four years, winning a total of 42 races in 1966, 1968 and 1969. He remained a force in NASCAR well into the 1970s, reaching double digits in victories in 1973 and 1976. Pearson was a fan favorite, but he was never really comfortable with life as a sports celebrity. While other drivers embraced the spotlight, he tried his best to keep a low profile.

Versatile and multi-talented David Pearson, a threat to win any race he entered during the 1960s

The big star of the circuit during the 1960s (and 1970s, for that matter) was Richard Petty—"The King." He literally grew up with NASCAR, working in the pits for his father, Lee. He watched and learned everything about the racing business. By the time Petty joined the circuit as a driver in 1958 his head contained the combined knowledge of a top mechanic and wheelman, and he had also absorbed the vision of people like Bill France. Petty won Rookie of the Year honors in 1959, the same year his father captured his third NASCAR championship. He would have won his first race that year, too, were it not for a protest lodged by his dad! That level of competitiveness drove the Pettys, who reversed roles after Lee stopped driving in the early 1960s and became Richard's man in the pits.

Petty established himself as a top driver by his 21st birthday, finishing second in points in 1960 and coming in first, second, or third an amazing eight times during the

Lee and Richard Petty in 1967. The father-and-son team produced a record 27 victories that year.

1960s. In 1967 he had a season for the ages, winning 27 times in 49 starts and finishing second in seven other races. That began an unbroken string of double-digit victories that ran through the 1971 season. His consistency was remarkable. Petty had his down periods like other drivers, but unlike his peers they rarely lasted more than a few races. The teamwork and creative thinking he had learned as a teenager became the hallmark of the Petty crew, and he made sure that his support team was well-paid and highly publicized. The fierce loyalty this bred enabled him to stay on top of the NASCAR scene for 20 years, during which he won 200 races.

NASCAR's decade of radical growth was not without its growing pains. But each time a crisis developed, Bill France took charge. In the early 1960s, the Charlotte superspeedway, which was operated by driver Curtis Turner, was underfinanced and poorly run. Turner approached the Teamsters union, which had been hoping to organize NASCAR drivers and thus cut themselves in on a growing business. France, horrified by this thought, suspended Turner and partner Tim Flock from NASCAR for four years, then saw to it personally that Charlotte got moving toward profitability.

In 1963 Ford and Chrysler, companies that had bailed out of NASCAR sponsorship after the 1957 Martinsville crash, decided to get back into racing. Along with tire manufacturers Goodyear and Firestone, these two giants pumped hundreds of millions of dollars into making their products better and better. They bristled whenever France altered the rules to maintain overall competitiveness—Ford would accuse him of favoring Chrysler, and vice versa. By 1969, the quest for speed between Ford and Chrysler had gotten out of hand. They were hiring the best drivers, mechanics, engineers, and designers for the sole purpose of beating each other on the racing circuit. The drivers began to worry that perhaps their safety was being ignored in the name of winning. Speeds were approaching 200 miles an hour, and these were basically showroom cars—one slip, one flinch, one blown tire was all it took to turn a bumper-to-bumper race into a graveyard. The drivers revolted prior to the opening of the Talladega Speedway in September 1969, claiming it was too dangerous. This was a direct challenge to France, who had ordered the track to be built for speed.

Was NASCAR, with its network of racetracks, in charge of the sport? Or did the drivers hold all the cards? The automobile and tire manufacturers watched with intense interest. If the race were called off, or if fans did not show up, that would break NASCAR's monopoly on stock-car racing and force France out of the picture. Then the manufacturers would be able to move in and reorganize the sport in a way that best suited their needs. Richard Petty organized a boycott of the race, and all but one of the Top 20 drivers stayed away.

As always, France acted swiftly and decisively. He gathered the press at Talladega, wedged his hulking 60-year-old frame into a car, and took off around the track. Before anyone knew what was happening, he was hurtling across the asphalt at more than 175 mph. It was an ingenious ploy—obviously, if a fat old man could negotiate this "dangerous" track at 175, the top drivers could surely survive going 190. The race went on as scheduled, and although it was not a sell-out, enough fans showed up for France to make his point: mess with NASCAR, and you mess with me; mess with me, and you will lose.

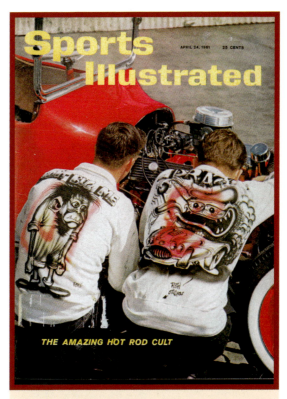

Hot-rodders even had their shirts customized, as this 1961 **Sports Illustrated** shows.

Drag Racing's 1960s Heyday

By the 1960s, drag racing had become a full-fledged American subculture, with its own look, its own language, and some of the best nicknames in all of sports. There was Don "Big Daddy" Garlits and his Swamp Rat, Tony "Loner" Nancy and his Wedge, Chris "The Mad Greek" Karamesines and his Chizler, and John "Dusty" Rhodes and his Rhodes' Runner.

Among all these characters there were two who engaged the fans like no others during the decade—Don Prudhomme and

Tom McEwen. Top drivers on the circuit, both had won national championships. Prudhomme, who was nicknamed "the Snake," always seemed to get more attention—perhaps because he was tall and handsome, and drove the instantly recognizable "Hawaiian" for famed owner Roland Leong. This made McEwen crazy. The owner of a supersized ego, he hated to be upstaged. So McEwen did a little research and decided to call himself the "Mongoose"—the snake's mortal enemy. Their weekly battles drew thousands of new fans to drag racing every year. In 1966, Prudhomme left Leong to build his own car, and he was replaced by a cocky 22-year-old

Don "The Snake" Prudhomme. He and his famous Hawaiian were the most instantly recognizable car-and-driver combination of the 1960s.

another milestone when he became the NHRA's first two-time champ. In between he became the first driver to crack the 200-mph barrier, reaching the double-century mark at the Detroit Dragway. The key to Garlits's record-breaking was the quick start provided by his new M&H Racemaster tires. It was not the first time he had tried something new to gain an edge against the competition, and it was certainly not his first contribution to the sport. Garlits was responsible for the rear-engine hot rod. He came up with the idea after suffering a terrible accident early in his career. His motor exploded during a race and blanketed him in flames. After Garlits recovered, he designed a dragster with the engine situated behind

named Mike Snively, who became the sport's Top Eliminator in the Hawaiian.

Although Top Fuel dragsters were the highlight of most meets, during the 1960s, the stock-car category also got much attention. Arnie "Farmer" Beswick reached 101.89 mph at the 1960 World Series of Drag Racing, and five years later Shirley Shahan, a 27-year-old mother of three, proved hot rodding was not just for men when she became Top Stock Eliminator in her "Drag-On Lady."

The most significant story of the 1960s, however, was the genius and daring of Don Garlits. In 1963 he became the man to beat when he finished as the Top Eliminator for fuel dragsters at the NHRA Winternationals. Four years later, Big Daddy reached

Tom "The Mongoose" McEwen, Prudhomme's arch rival. McEwen continued to race—and win—right into the 1990s.

Don "Big Daddy" Garlits, behind the wheel of an old front-engine dragster in 1964

the driver, thus providing greater safety. Known as the sport's great experimenter, he would further build on this reputation during the 1970s.

As the 1960s drew to a close, drag racing stood poised to become a major sport. It had gained official recognition from the Fédération Internationale de l'Automobile, and its new wheelie-popping "Funny Car" division was a smash hit with fans. Still, few imagined how popular and sophisticated the sport was about to become.

Grand Prix Racing: The 1970s

The 1970 Formula One season offered fans more than a dozen sophisticated new cars, as well as a rising star in Jochen Rindt. The Austrian star scored a dramatic victory at the Monaco Grand Prix in his new Lotus 72,

and took the checkered flag at the Belgian, French, British, and German Grands Prix. A great career was cut short, however, during practice for the Italian Grand Prix. Rindt's brake shaft snapped and he slammed into a concrete support, dying on impact. Earlier in the year, the beloved Bruce McLaren lost his life testing a new sports car. Its hood flew up, he could not see where he was going, and he crashed. In a year tinged with sadness, the final irony came when a rookie named Emerson Fittipaldi won the season's final race in a Lotus 72. The victory denied Jacky Ickx the World Championship, and gave the title posthumously to Fittipaldi's fallen teammate, Rindt. With a sudden void among the world's top drivers, fans wondered whether a newcomer or a veteran would step up to fill it.

The answer came from Jackie Stewart, who took this opportunity to dominate the

THE KING

Richard Petty's main contributions to the rapid rise of stock-car racing in the 1960s went well beyond the 101 victories he chalked up during the decade. His fearless-yet-intelligent style set the standard for the era. The men who had come up during the early days of NASCAR were often reckless drivers, and as speed increased on the circuit, many of them—including Weatherly and Roberts—died in horrible wrecks. Petty, on the other hand, was rarely involved in collisions, yet there he was week after week, at or near the front of the pack. The Petty team, meanwhile, gave all the other owners something to shoot for. Other crews watched in awe as Petty completed pit stops in half the time it took everyone else, and marveled at the subtle mechanical improvements that originated from his garage. Off the track, Petty was always available to his fans, scribbling his regal signature for hours before and after a race. Had he withdrawn from his admirers—or turned down interviews from the newspapers and magazines—other drivers surely would have followed suit, and that would have been devastating to the sport's growth. To this day, there is an unwritten rule among NASCAR drivers that you get out and connect with the fans.

Formula One circuit. In 1963, Ken Tyrell had founded Tyrell Racing and hired Stewart, then an unknown Scottish driver. The two had risen to fame together, and Stewart had turned down huge offers from other teams out of loyalty. This loyalty paid off in 1971, when Tyrell unveiled his new 001. The car had been tested in a wind tunnel to achieve the best overall shape. This included a spade-like front airfoil and fuel tanks on either side of the driver, as well as double disc brakes. This combination produced incredible handling, while the newest Cosworth engine supplied plenty of power. Stewart won the Spanish Grand Prix, Monaco Grand Prix, French Grand Prix, British Grand Prix, German Grand Prix, and Canadian Grand Prix, with teammate Francois Cevert taking two seconds and winning the season's final race, the U.S. Grand Prix. In 1972 Stewart continued to drive well, winning the Argentinian Grand Prix, the French Grand Prix, the Canadian Grand Prix, and the U.S. Grand Prix.

The big surprise of the early 1970s was Fittipaldi, whose 1972 season actually eclipsed Stewart's. The 25-year-old Brazilian won in Spain and Belgium, then outdueled Stewart at the British Grand Prix. A victory in the Austrian Grand Prix gave him the edge over Stewart in the quest for the World Championship, which Fittipaldi nailed down when he beat a bunch of high-powered Ferraris in their own backyard at the Italian Grand Prix.

Fittipaldi was not the only significant

newcomer to the Grand Prix circuit in the early 1970s. Corporate sponsors flocked to the sport during this period, creating more teams with more cars, and thus more opportunities for hot young drivers. Moving up from Formula Two were South African Jody Sheckter for McLaren, and Austrian Niki Lauda for March Engineering, a new company formed in England with the backing of Andy Granatelli. Coming over from America were familiar Indy faces Pete Revson for McLaren, Mario Andretti for Ferrari, and Mark Donohue for Penske.

The mid-1970s saw the Grand Prix schedule expand to 15 races. Following Fittipaldi's first driving title, Brazil created a new race to take advantage of the explosion of national interest in auto racing. As expected, Fittipaldi won both South American races in 1973, throwing down the gauntlet for another duel with Stewart. The Scotsman responded by taking the South African and Belgian Grand Prixes, and edging Fittipaldi at Monaco by one second to tie Jim Clark for the all-time lead in Grand Prix victories with 25. Stewart moved into first place—and won his third World Championship—by driving to easy victories at the Dutch Grand Prix and German Grand Prix. Stewart's record is considered one of the most remarkable feats in auto-racing history. Driving at a time when everyone was using essentially the same engine, he had to rely on his skill, guile, and instincts to win, whereas Clark had the advantage of a superior Lotus for much of his career. Stewart's wonderful season ended with profound sadness, though, when teammate Cevert was killed during the U.S. Grand Prix. Stewart retired, never to take the wheel again. That seemed to leave Fittipaldi as the unchallenged king of the road.

Feeling Lotus was losing its edge, Fittipaldi left in 1974 to join McLaren and drive the M23, which many believed to be the top car on the circuit. Emmo won his second World Championship with victories in Brazil, Belgium, and Canada, but it was not a title easily won. He and Niki Lauda ran neck-and-neck in driving points all season long. Lauda's Ferrari 312B3 proved to be the faster car, but in the end its unreliability cost him the title. The Austrian star got a redesigned 312 the following year, and drove it like he and the car were one. Lauda outlasted Fittipaldi at the Monaco Grand Prix, and cruised to wins in Belgium, Sweden, France, and the United States. Fittipaldi had another excellent season, but could not catch Lauda.

The 1976 season saw the rise of James Hunt, for years the top driver for BRM. When the company decided to pull out of Formula One, he was left without a ride. With Fittipaldi having left McLaren to form his own team with his brother, Wilson, Hunt found a new home. There he flourished as McLaren's number-one man, winning the World Championship by a single point. It was a title that would not have been possible without a terrible mishap at the German Grand Prix. Lauda—who was leading all drivers in points—hit a wet patch at 150 mph and bounced around the course like a pinball. Two cars struck him and his car burst into flames. Lauda's fellow drivers stopped their cars, jumped out and pulled him from the inferno, but he was already badly burned and had inhaled poisonous fumes. As he lay in the hospital, doctors gave him no chance of surviving. He was even given his last rites. But then Lauda began a miraculous recovery. Against doctor's orders and common sense, he even returned

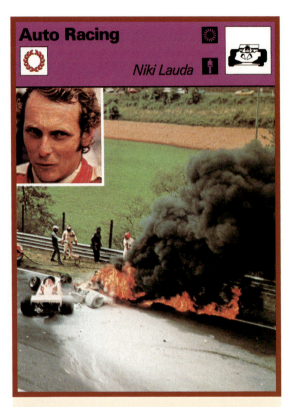

Auto Racing

Niki Lauda

This is one card Niki Lauda probably does not have in his collection. It depicts the crash that nearly killed him in 1976.

advantage of this new feature. Chapman's partner in this revolutionary experiment was Mario Andretti, who had joined Lotus in 1976 when he heard about plans for the 78. Not since Jim Clark had Chapman worked as closely (or as well) with a driver in the development of a car. Andretti said the Lotus 78 handled as if it were painted to the road. The term "ground effects" would soon become part of racing language.

Chapman's new design dominated Formula One racing. In 1978, Andretti and teammate Ronnie Peterson vied for the World Championship all season long. Andretti won, but not the way he wanted to. At the Italian Grand Prix, Peterson was involved in a pileup and his car was pushed underneath a barrier. His lower body was crushed and he died in the hospital that evening. In 1979, Lotus failed to win a race, but that was only because everyone had successfully followed Chapman's lead. As the turbo era dawned on Grand Prix racing, two new stars came to the fore for Ferrari: the South African, Jodi Sheckter, and Canada's Gilles Villeneuve. The timing could not have been better for Ferrari, which lost Lauda to retirement in 1979. Scheckter and Villeneuve would keep Ferrari in the headlines for a long, long time.

to racing that season. One of the most unforgettable sights of the decade was Lauda, still unhealed, showing up at the Italian Grand Prix. Incredibly, he finished fourth!

Lauda returned to the circuit and won his second World Championship in 1977, but the big news was a comeback by Lotus. Colin Chapman had worked for almost two years on his new 78 model, a car he believed would revolutionize the sport. Taking a cue from Tyrell, he logged hundreds of hours in a wind tunnel, tweaking the car's shape until he came up with what he was after: an upside-down wing design that created a vacuum under the body and actually "sucked" the car to the road. He then had Goodyear design special tires to take full

Indy-Car Racing in the 1970s: Farewell to Offy

The 1970 Indianapolis 500 marked the first time the race's total purse exceeded $1 million. The race was won by Al Unser, who was in the midst of a remarkable streak. After recovering from a motorcycle accident in 1969, he won 15 of the 24 Indy car races he entered, and also took the National Dirt

Action from the Monaco Grand Prix shows the low-to-the-pavement "ground effects" design that dominated Formula One racing in the late 1970s.

Track championship. The younger brother of 1967 Indy winner Bobby Unser, Al was the rising star of one of the most celebrated racing families. He won again in 1971, fending off challenges from a group of powerful M16 McLarens with new turbocharged engines. As the next few years would prove, this was quite an accomplishment.

Bobby Unser, driving one of Dan Gurney's turbocharged Eagles, achieved a qualifying speed of 196 mph in 1972—more than 17 mph faster than the previous mark.

But it was one of the distinctive, wedge-shaped McLarens, driven by Mark Donohue, that took the checkered flag. By 1973, every car in the race was turbocharged, and lap speeds approached 200 mph for the first time. Johnny Rutherford won for McLaren in 1974, and Bobby Unser took the checkered flag in 1975, giving car owner Dan Gurney his first 500 win.

Offenhausers were the engines of choice at Indy during the mid-1970s, but they were not without competition. A. J. Foyt had purchased Ford's V-8 motors when Henry Ford II decided to get his company out of racing, and although they produced a bit less power than the Offys, their peak output was right around the limit set in 1974 for Indy cars. About a third of the top drivers went for the Foyt engines, including Foyt himself, who desperately wanted to become the first four-time winner of the Indianapolis 500. He accomplished this in 1977, when he ran a magnificent race start-to-finish. The victory made Foyt the toast of the American racing scene (he had already scored a second-place finish at the Daytona 500 that spring), and he earned the distinction of becoming the first driver to top the $1-million mark in career earnings at Indianapolis.

As the 1970s came to an end, engine aficionados had plenty to think about. The fastest qualifiers for the 1978 Indy 500—and the winner, Al Unser—had neither Offenhauser nor Foyt engines. Their cars contained Cosworth motors, which achieved speeds well in excess of 200 mph. In 1979, Rick Mears won in a Cosworth-powered car built by Roger Penske. Within a couple of years, Offy engines would disappear forever from the 500. Also, "ground-effects" cars, after the model developed by

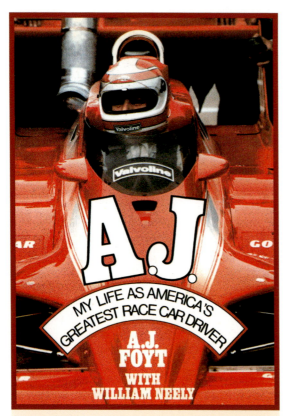

A.J. Foyt's autobiography was a winner among racing fans in 1983. Foyt himself was a winner that year, taking Le Mans at the age of 48.

Lotus's Colin Chapman and Mario Andretti for Formula One racing, were on their way to Indy. Indeed, another British invasion seemed imminent.

NASCAR Racing: The 1970s

With the drivers back in line for the 1970 season, Bill France set his sights on teaching the automobile manufacturers a lesson. The one area of NASCAR where he had always enjoyed unchallenged control was in the garages. Whatever rules and restrictions France placed on cars had to be followed to

the letter. For the 1970 season, he required all cars to install a device called a restrictor plate. Located in the carburetor, it controlled the flow of fuel into an engine, and thus limited how much power an engine could produce. This effectively counteracted everything the manufacturers had done to make their cars faster, and won back the loyalty of many of the NASCAR drivers who had left the fold in 1969. Within a few years, the frustrated car companies started drifting away from the sport, opting to spend their money on government-mandated pollution and safety research.

France had won another round, and NASCAR was back in total control of stock-car racing. That was important, because in 1972 France finally stepped down as head of NASCAR, turning the reins over to his son, Bill Jr. By ensuring that the cars were as evenly matched as possible, France knew the sport could now refocus on what had brought it to national prominence: the drivers.

And what drivers they were. Every race seemed to come down to a battle involving Richard Petty, David Pearson, Cale Yarborough, and Bobby Allison. And when any of these fierce competitors slipped back, drivers like Buddy Baker, Benny Parsons, James Hylton, and Donnie Allison were usually there to challenge. NASCAR fans were also treated to Indy legend A. J. Foyt, who usually entered around six races a year. Far from a novelty act, Foyt won five events between 1970 and 1972, including the Daytona 500. Petty remained the king of stock-car racing, taking the Grand National title—which was renamed the Winston Cup Championship in 1971—in 1971, 1972, 1974, 1975, and 1979. Pearson remained a force right through the decade, and although he did not win another driving championship, he did win more races than anyone else in 1973 and again in 1976.

The most notable new star was Yarborough, who had been kicking around the circuit for more than a decade. During the late 1960s, when lap speeds increased so dramatically, Yarborough won his first bit of fame, taking six races in 1968. But he faded from the scene after the speeds dropped and sanity once again prevailed at NASCAR. Yarborough was not a big fan of sanity. He was a throwback to the thrill-seeking, risk-taking "good ol' boys" of the 1940s and 1950s. No one pushed his car harder, and no one put more faith in his car. This combination resulted in some major crack-ups, but it also translated into major wins. The fans adored Yarborough, and his fellow racers admired his spirit, even if it did lead to an occasional fistfight. He tied Petty for most

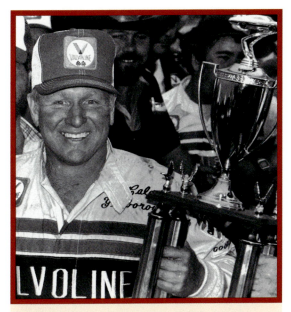

Cale Yarborough, whose fearless driving first paid off when NASCAR lap speeds began to rise in the late 1960s

wins during the 1974 season, and began attracting major sponsorship money. With a hot car and a crew capable of keeping him under control, he was NASCAR champ from 1976 to 1978, and continued winning through the early 1980s.

That did not leave much left for Bobby Allison, who gained a reputation as NASCAR's annual runner-up. Five times he finished second in points, not winning a championship until 1983, when he was 46 years old. During the 1970s, though, he was right in the thick of things every week. In 1970, he finished in the top four 30 times, and in 1971 he won 10 races—more than any other driver. Allison was a racing fanatic, often entering dirt-track events on the weekends when there was nothing doing at NASCAR, and winning NASCAR events right up until an accident ended his career at age 51.

The 1970s closed out in grand style, with a couple of hot-shot newcomers capturing the imagination of fans. Dale Earnhardt and Darrell Waltrip made their presence known, with Earnhardt winning 1979 Rookie of the Year honors and Waltrip—who captured 19 races from 1977 to 1979—showing no respect for his elders either on or off the track. This pair would usher in a new era during the 1980s, ending the stranglehold of the veterans who had brought the sport so far during the 1960s and 1970s.

Drag Racing in the 1970s: Big Daddy & Cha Cha

The 1970s were a time of turmoil, disillusionment, and conflict in the United States. Yet somehow, drag racing stayed almost completely unaffected. Perhaps it was mov-

ing too fast to notice. Or maybe it was too deeply rooted in a simpler, more innocent America to be swayed by the winds of change. Drag racing's loyal fans and participants clung to their small-town pride and that "I'll get you next time" spirit of competition that had drawn so many to the sport in the first place. It was nice to find a place where things were still settled the old-fashioned way.

If an event was washed out by a storm, everyone would convene at the nearest high school gymnasium or local recreation hall and an impromptu picnic would be slapped together, with plenty of beer and barbecue on hand. Fans could even get in on a little "bench racing," as drivers and mechanics traded tips, insults, and predictions. It sounds like a scene right out of the 1950s, but this kind of camaraderie characterized the drag racing-community right through the 1970s.

Drag racing was not, however, stuck in time. The sport had grown steadily during the 1960s and interest was now widespread, thanks in large part to the efforts of the NHRA. The association now boasted seven categories of cars that competed in a series of 35 regional meets throughout the year. The goal of all drivers was to make it to the NHRA's World Finals, where the Top Eliminator in each division was decided. Automotive technology was also advancing at a rapid pace. Top Fuel cars—the long, rear-engine dragsters—were now easily surpassing 200 mph and covering a quarter mile in less than six seconds.

The driver most associated with this period in drag racing is Don Garlits. He had pioneered a great many of the engineering breakthroughs in the sport, and he continued as hot-rodding's master innovator in the 1970s. Garlits installed an air spoiler on a dragster before anyone else, and spearheaded the use of port injection. The first driver to reach 200 mph and 250 mph in a dragster, he accumulated trophies like most kids collect baseball cards. He won 112 national events during his career and claimed the Top Fuel world championship titles 17 times. He was the racer every other driver gunned for. Indeed, beating Big Daddy even once was enough to make a driver's career.

Garlits was not just out for himself—he wanted the sport to grow, and his fellow racers to receive fair compensation. In 1972 he struck a nerve with the NHRA when he started a rival sanctioning body called the Professional Racers' Association. Garlits was upset with the lack of prize money in the sport. NHRA champions were still making less than $7,000 for winning the nationals and that did not seem right to him. Considering the popularity of the sport— thousands of fans attended regional meets, while even bigger crowds showed up for national events—he did not see why drivers received such puny prizes. In the first meet sponsored by the PRA, Garlits offered a purse of $25,000 to the winner of each division. The NHRA got the message, and the following year more than doubled its prize money.

By the mid-1970s, Garlits might have chosen to make a quiet exit from the sport, or at least assume a low-profile, behind-the-scenes role. But in the 1970s another driver came along who drove him absolutely crazy. Her name was Shirley "Cha Cha" Muldowney, and she irritated Garlits more than an engine failure on the starting line. She was the first woman ever licensed by the NHRA to drive a Top Fuel dragster, and won her first of three Top Fuel titles in 1977; over her career she would drive her hot-pink machine to 17 NHRA titles.

The daughter of a professional boxer, Muldowney inherited all of her dad's combativeness. She learned to drive at the age of 12 in her home town of Schenectady, New York, and was running in drag races by 16. Picked on a lot in her youth, she was all too ready to take a swing at anyone who doubted her or put her down. As she liked to say, kicking butt was her specialty—both on and off the track. Early in her career she was burned badly in a crash. Her goggles melted onto her face and singed her eyes shut. Plastic surgery covered the scars, but Muldowney still hated to be seen without makeup.

What irked Garlits and the other drivers most about Muldowney was that, despite racing in a man's world, she demanded to

Shirley "Cha Cha" Muldowney, who combined skill and attitude to win 17 NHRA titles.

REVOLUTION!

During the 1970s, several top Indy car drivers decided that the United States Auto Club (USAC)—which had taken over from the AAA in the mid-1950s as the governing body of American racing—had lost touch with their sport, and attempted to gain control of racing by creating CART, which stood for Championship Auto Racing Teams. CART set up a rival series of Indy car races. This infuriated the USAC, which responded by banning CART drivers (including the Unsers, Gordon Johncock, and Danny Ongais) from its events. In turn, these drivers went to court and won a restraint of trade decision against USAC, and were allowed to race again. With power in American racing divided—and sponsorship dollars pouring in from corporate sponsors—fans sensed some major changes were coming to their sport.

be treated like a lady—and had a habit of getting in people's faces if they did not comply. She and Garlits, in particular, despised each other. Garlits was a self-proclaimed "male chauvinist pig" who felt a woman's place was in the kitchen, not the driver's seat of a hot rod. He also attacked Muldowney for knowing nothing about the mechanical workings of a car. She was simply a driver, and he could not respect that. They waged legendary battles right into the 1980s, attracting much attention and drawing thousands of new fans to the sport. Spectators marveled at how Muldowney's incredible reflexes got her off the line faster than anyone else on the circuit, enabling her to beat cars that were clearly faster than her own. To the unending frustration of Big Daddy, she defeated him far more than half the time they raced.

Muldowney never got the upper hand in one area, though, and that was sponsorship money. There was not a lot of it in drag racing to begin with, and what little there was

tended to go toward the male Top Fuel drivers. During the 1970s, Top Fuel endorsement money was watered down further by the rise of the Funny Car division, which actually surpassed Top Fuel as drag racing's number-one attraction. Fans loved everything about Funny Cars. They were not as fast as Top Fuel dragsters, but their unique appearance more than made up for their slower speeds. Also, something strange always seemed to happen when Funny Cars raced. Partly because of their distinctive design—the front of the car hanging unusually low and the rear sticking up high—they were extraordinarily difficult to handle. They skidded and lurched down the raceway, and sometimes became airborne by the end of a run. Sponsors liked Funny Cars because, unlike the bare-bones Top Fuel cars, there were a lot of places to stick a big, eye-catching logo.

The first racer to fully appreciate the potential of Funny Cars was Kenny Bernstein. The son of a department-store manager in

Texas, Bernstein learned the value of good promotional skills at an early age. When he was nine he convinced his father to let him sell socks to browsing shoppers. The kid was a natural. At about the same age Bernstein was introduced to cars. He was hooked immediately, and began racing as a teenager. When he left for college, he even brought his dragster along with him.

Bernstein dropped out of school in 1966 to pursue a career in drag racing. Over the next dozen years he quit and returned to the sport on a number of occasions. Unlike other hot-rodders, he had money, and he also possessed a special flair for creating profitable businesses when he was not racing—including a sandwich shop that blossomed into 17 franchise locations. Bernstein's magic touch finally began to pay dividends in drag racing in 1978. He bought a Funny Car and named it after his best-selling sandwich, the Chelsea King. In 1979, Bernstein won the International Hot Rod Association's Funny Car championship. Then he hit on an idea. He drove to St. Louis and convinced Anheuser-Busch, which makes Budweiser beer, to sponsor his car. The company liked the idea, and Bernstein then did something that would alter his sport forever. He changed the name of his car to the "Budweiser King." As the decade ended, a new era of corporate sponsorship in drag racing was about to begin.

Grand Prix Racing 1980–86: Formula One Goes High-Tech

The coming of the turbocharged engine to the Formula One circuit was not a development the British racing teams liked to see. These engines were complicated to build and extremely expensive, which gave the edge in research and development to the automobile manufacturers. Indeed, at the start of the 1980s, several well-known names in the Grand Prix business—including McLaren, Tyrell, and Lotus—were already beginning to feel the financial squeeze of staying up-to-date. To make matters worse for the independent car builders, the aerodynamic "skirts" developed by Colin Chapman to create ground effects were under fire by the Fédération Internationale du Sport Automobile (FISA). This meant they would have no way to counter advances made by the cash-rich Renault, Ferrari, and Alfa Romeo factories, which were busily developing wonderful new engines.

The Formula One Constructors Association (FOCA)—the organization that represented the needs of the "kit-car" garages—threatened to break off and run its own races. Against this backdrop, Nelson Piquet and Alan Jones, both driving British cars, dueled right down to the season's final race for the 1980 driver's championship. Jones won after the two collided going into the first corner and Piquet could not restart his car. When the 1981 season began, the split between FISA and FOCA was starting to scare away Grand Prix sponsors, which did not help anyone's cause.

An agreement was reached whereby FISA would remain the sport's governing body, but FOCA would have control over key financial matters, including negotiations with race promoters and television companies. While this deal was being hammered out, Jones won the South African Grand Prix, but because it did not include drivers loyal to FISA, he was not awarded any Grand Prix points. This would come into play on the season's final day, when he won a race in Las Vegas but actually lost the World Championship to fifth-place finisher Piquet by one point. Had Jones been given some credit for his win in South Africa, he would have had a second-straight championship. Fed up with the politics of racing, he retired and headed home to Australia.

Despite some minor glitches it was, on the whole, an excellent year for the British shops. They had made their point with FISA, won some concessions on the issue of skirts, and the two top drivers were winning with Cosworth engines. But they knew that advantage would not last much longer, and many garages began shopping around for turbocharged engines. Turbos had been winning oval-track races for more than a decade, but weren't responsive and efficient enough to handle the sudden speed changes of Grand Prix racing. By 1983, however, the mechanics had fine-tuned the turbocharged engine's performance to the point that it had become the winning engine in Formula One—and would remain so through the rest of the decade. The independent teams managed to secure the new engines and thus remained competitive, and the sport was able to set out on a new course. Piquet, driving a turbocharged Brabham— the first of the small teams to switch over— had a smashing year in 1983. He captured the Brazilian Grand Prix, Italian Grand Prix, European Grand Prix, and South African Grand Prix to beat out Renault's Alain Prost for the World Championship.

With the Grand Prix circuit fully turbocharged, FISA issued new regulations to ensure that the added power did not have tragic consequences. The organization curbed refueling stops, forcing drivers to use their gas-guzzling turbochargers only when needed. This spurred improvements in the electronic sensors that managed the engine, bringing racing one more step into the computer age. If a car could be set up to take only the fuel it needed onto the course, it would not be weighed down by "safety" gas, and thus would have an important advantage. Within a couple of years, these sensors became so accurate that drivers would be running out of gas just as they crossed the finish line!

The irony in all of this progress was that Renault, which had introduced turbocharging to Formula One back in the late 1970s, could not seem to win anything. The company took out its frustration on its top driver, Prost, and fired him. He was immediately snapped up by McLaren, which had lured Niki Lauda out of retirement. McLaren had quite a package, with two top drivers, rich sponsors, a great fuel-management system made by Bosch, and the very best Michelin tires.

Not surprisingly, the 1984 championship came down to the final race, in Portugal, with Lauda and Prost neck-and-neck. Prost won but Lauda finished second— enough to make him the racing world's comeback king by a half-point. Prost rebounded to win the 1985 title (his first of two straight), but it was a season most notable for the first Grand Prix wins by two special young drivers, Nigel Mansell and Ayrton Senna. In the second race of 1986, one hundredth of a second separated the two at the finish line.

Grand-Prix Racing 1987–89: Star Power

Mansell and Senna represented a different breed of driver. They looked at the huge paychecks they were pulling down and,

Alain Prost driving for McLaren in 1988. He and teammate Ayrton Senna won a total of 15 races that season.

quite understandably, believed themselves to be superstars. And they were treated as such by their crews, their sponsors, and their fans. These were turbocharged athletes driving turbocharged machines, and they had only one thing in mind when they squeezed into the cockpit: winning. On the balance, this was a good thing; bigger-than-life drivers drew new fans and sponsors to Formula One.

But it did have its drawbacks. When the veteran Nelson Piquet was lured away from Brabham by Williams, he replaced young Mansell as the team's number-one driver. In the past, this would have meant that Piquet would be protected and helped by his teammate during a race. Mansell, however, did not subscribe to such chivalrous notions, and he infuriated the former world champion by treating him like the enemy. Senna, meanwhile, actually drove his number-two man off the Lotus team, then blocked the appointment of the talented Derek Warwick. Senna lobbied successfully for a

lesser Formula Three driver whom he knew would not pose a threat to his dominant position. Besides the personality conflicts that developed, the new "star system" also diverted millions of dollars needed for automotive development directly into the pockets of the drivers. That meant that many teams could no longer afford to come out with a brand-new car each year.

Another new and considerable expense in Formula One racing was the growing practice of designing engines specifically for qualifying. Starting in the first or second row was more important than ever, so for the two or three laps required to record a top qualifying speed, some companies resorted to special turbocharged engines so powerful that they literally destroyed themselves after a few minutes! The rich teams thus gained a big advantage over the poorer ones, but by resorting to these methods the rich teams were getting poorer with every race. Finally, FISA stepped in and announced that it would phase out supercharging by the end of the decade—everyone would have to switch back to the "normally aspirated" cars. This was bad news for companies like Honda and Renault, which had sunk untold millions into their supercharger projects, and great news for Cosworth, whose V-8 had all but disappeared from Grand Prix racing.

As the decade drew to a close, Senna joined Prost at McLaren to form an unprecedented one-two punch. In 1988, they finished first and second in 10 of the year's 16 races, and won a total of 15 between them, with Senna taking 8 and Prost 7. The next year, in the nonturbocharged car McLaren built for the new formula, the pair won 10 races, with Senna taking 6 and Prost 4. Their intense rivalry, however, nearly tore the McLaren team apart. Mansell, now driving for Ferrari, kept right on these two, but he came away with just two wins, unable to catch the world's fastest cars.

Indy-Car Racing: The 1980s

The rise of FOCA in Grand Prix racing during the 1980s was mirrored by the growing influence of CART in the world of Indy cars. The most noticeable change was in the size of the purses, especially at the Indianapolis 500. From 1980 to 1986, prize money for the big race nearly tripled, reaching more than $4 million. Needless to say, the fierce competition that had long characterized the Indy 500 got even fiercer. Johnny Rutherford opened up the decade with his third Indy win, driving a full ground-effects car built by Chaparral. He held off challenges from Bobby Unser and Mario Andretti, each driving cars for the dominant Penske team. Both teams used

Cosworth engines, and throughout the 1980s they would power the most successful Indy cars.

Bobby Unser came back to win in 1981, giving him an Indy crown in the 1960s, 1970s, and 1980s. In 1983, a controversy arose when Al Unser, Jr.—driving in his first 500 and several laps off the lead—tried to block Tom Sneva, who was attempting to challenge Al Unser, Sr., for the lead. Sneva managed to pass both Unsers and win the race. Brash young Al Jr. would raise the ire of many in the Indy world, but ultimately he proved worthy of his family heritage. Meanwhile, Penske team drivers scored victories three more times during the decade, with Rick Mears taking the flag in 1984 and 1988, and Danny Sullivan winning in 1985. Sullivan's victory illustrated just how competitive the Indianapolis 500 had become. In an attempt to pass leader Mario Andretti, the 25-year-old Sullivan took his multimillion-dollar racer through a turn so low that he bounced across the "rumble strip" marking the inner edge of track. When he came back on to the track, he spun out in front of Andretti at 200 mph, nearly causing a major crash. Incredibly, with 12 laps to go Sullivan made the same crazy move again and this time took the lead. He won the race by a couple of seconds.

Indeed, so much cash was now at stake that drivers took chances they never would have considered a few years earlier. When Bobby Rahal won the 1986 race, he pocketed more than half a million dollars for first prize, and earned an additional million dollars from incentive-rich endorsement deals. In 1984, Emerson Fittipaldi was lured out of retirement by the rich winner's checks on the Indy car circuit. He finished second in the 1985 Indy 500, won the race in 1989,

Bobby Rahal, on his way to a $1.5-million payday at the 1986 Indy 500

and remained one of the sport's top drivers right into the 1990s.

In the final years of the 1980s, Indy-car racing had completed a transformation begun a decade earlier, when CART first challenged the supremacy of the USAC. It had become a sport run by entrepreneurial team owners, more so even than the Grand Prix circuit. The leader of this group was the man who led the initial break from the USAC, Roger Penske. Each year he cut new deals with sponsors, shopped the world for the best car components, built the fastest cars, and hired the top people to drive them. The 1988 race featured his cars in each of the three spots on the front row. Though less of an advantage than in Grand Prix racing, it was nonetheless a symbolic tribute to Penske, who lit the way for so many during the 1980s.

NASCAR Racing: The 1980s

The 1980s saw stock-car racing equal and then surpass Indy-car racing as America's favorite four-wheel sport. The formula for success was a combination of close, entertaining races and a mix of personalities that gave each race its own unique story line. From the sport's amazing growth in the 1970s, NASCAR had learned that the quest for speed took a backseat to "putting on a show"—before, during, after, and in be-

Roger Penske, the man credited by many for bringing auto racing into the modern age

THE INTIMIDATOR

Richard Petty may forever be "the King" of stock car-racing, but fans of Dale Earnhardt claim no driver embodies the sport the way he does. The son of a dirt-track driver, Earnhardt has always lived by three words his father drummed into his head: "Establish your territory." He joined the NASCAR circuit as a full-timer in 1979 and won the championship in 1980, 1986, 1987, 1990, 1991, and 1994.

Earnhardt quickly became known as "the Intimidator" for his fearless, aggressive driving. Those who got in his way paid the price, often finding themselves squashed against the wall. Those who tried to run him down got the ride of their lives. Earnhardt grew up around racetracks, and watched his father struggle to keep his car on the road and earn enough money to keep his family fed. Ralph Earnhardt was just beginning to make some money at racing when he died of a heart attack while working on his car. Dale followed in his dad's footsteps and became a top dirt-track competitor. In 1979, he was hired by team owner Rod Osterlund to drive for him, and suddenly Earnhardt was in the big time. Using the same gritty style, he soon became a feared and respected competitor.

An old-time driver from an old-time racing family, Earnhardt proved to be entirely up-to-date when it came to marketing himself and the NASCAR circuit. As more and more young, good-looking drivers joined the circuit each year, he cast himself as a ruthless bully. Some fans adored him, while others reviled him. Either way, they came to see him race. In 1997, he became the first driver in any form of motor sport to surpass $30 million in career earnings, and has earned just as much from outside interests and endorsement deals.

tween each race. NASCAR saw to it that every event was closely contested. A steady stream of power restrictions continued throughout the decade, making it nearly impossible for one car to pull away from the pack. If a driver did build up a big lead, race officials would usually find a reason to wave a yellow caution flag, allowing other cars to pull into the pits and make the necessary adjustments to catch up.

In this regard, NASCAR was sometimes accused of purposely manipulating its races. But the throngs jamming the grandstands did not care. If they got to see a bumper-to-bumper finish, they went home happy. Some saw stock-car racing as a blend of Formula One and the World Wrestling Federation, but its growing legion of fans considered it a mix of high drama and good, clean fun. As always, the closeness between the drivers and fans fueled the sport. During the 1980s this approach was greatly enhanced by television, which gave NASCAR unprecedented coverage on network and cable TV.

As for drivers, the early 1980s signaled a changing of the guard, as Darrell Waltrip and Dale Earnhardt won the decade's first three Winston Cup championships and pretty much closed the book on the old-timers. Waltrip won again in 1985, then Earnhardt took the title in 1986 and 1987.

Coming on strong by the mid-1980s was Bill Elliott, who actually came to NASCAR at the same time as Waltrip and Earnhardt, but with far less fanfare. He led all drivers with 11 victories in 1985 and tied for the lead in 1988, when he won the Winston Cup championship. Elliott's 1985 performance made him an instant celebrity, for it included victories in the Daytona 500, Winston 500, and Southern 500—three of NASCAR's four big races. It also made him a rich man, as he became the first driver to win the "Winston Million" Award, which was accompanied by a seven-figure bonus check. Elliott handled his celebrity with grace and warmth, becoming the most uni-

versally admired driver to emerge during this time.

The Daytona 500, which had been won by seven different drivers during the 1970s, became the scene of some memorable performances during the 1980s. The circuit's veterans seemed to choose this race to let the young guys know they were still around, and it made for great story lines. In 1980, Buddy Baker, who had been a NASCAR fixture since 1959, achieved his last great victory with a win at Daytona. In 1981, Richard Petty won, capping off a career that had seen him win this event an amazing seven times. In 1983 and 1984, Cale Yarborough, who had cut his schedule down to 16 races a year, won the race in his mid-forties.

And in 1988, Bobby Allison scored the final victory of his career at Daytona in what many consider to be stock-car racing's finest performance of the 1980s. New restrictor-plate regulations brought the speed down by 15 mph, meaning skill and guile would count for more than usual. Allison, who was 50 years old, stayed right with the leaders. His son, Davey, was there, too, as

Bill Elliot, winner of the 1985 Daytona 500. The victory was one of 11 he scored that year.

father and son jockeyed for position with the ever-dangerous Waltrip. In the final laps, it was Davey first and Bobby second, and fans of the Allisons smiled knowingly at this "passing of the torch." That is, until Bobby shot past his 26-year-old boy to take the checkered flag!

Davey was no slouch. He captured NASCAR's fastest race, the Winston Select at Talladega, twice during the 1980s, and achieved a Top 10 ranking in 1988. Another "favorite son," Kyle Petty, became a full-time driver for Petty Enterprises in 1981. He went on to pass his dad in the year-end rankings in 1985, and became NASCAR's first third-generation winner when he took the checkered flag the following season in Richmond.

Among the other top drivers to break into the spotlight during the 1980s were Harry Gant, who won the Southern 500 at Darlington twice, and Rusty Wallace, who tied for the circuit lead in victories in 1988 and again in 1989, when he was crowned Winston Cup champion. Terry Labonte established himself as one of NASCAR's most consistent drivers when he edged Gant to capture the 1984 Winston Cup championship. He first came to the attention of racing fans when he won the 1980 Southern 500 at the age of 23, in just his second full season. Labonte was one of nine different winners of this race (NASCAR's oldest) during the 1980s, which gives some idea of the competitiveness this decade produced.

Indeed, it was by all measures quite a decade for NASCAR. As if by design, the Winston Cup championship went down to the final race each year from 1980 to 1984, bringing fan interest to a fever pitch. In 1989, Earnhardt won the final

race of the season to edge young upstarts Wallace and Mark Martin by the closest margin in Winston Cup history. Attendance at Winston Cup events soared, and by 1990 it was approaching 2 million. Products licensed by NASCAR, such as hats and T-shirts, were showing up all over the country. And a survey conducted in the mid-1980s revealed that nearly half of the adult fans of stock-car racing were women. Not surprisingly, the cigarette, soft drink, beer, and automotive product sponsors—whose logos traditionally covered most cars—soon found themselves competing for space with laundry detergents, panty hose, blue jeans, ketchup, and candy bars. Other American sports claimed to be family oriented, but NASCAR had the numbers to prove it.

Drag Racing 1980s: The Pro Stock Phenomenon

For most of the 1980s, Kenny Bernstein was the big man in drag racing. He became the first driver to break 260 mph and then 270 mph in a Funny Car, and won four consecutive national titles from 1985 to 1988. The big story, however, was the rise of the Pro Stock class. The lure of this classification was obvious. People liked to see cars that they could theoretically buy for themselves in an automobile showroom. It was what had always attracted people to NASCAR, and by the early 1980s the same dynamics were at work in the stock-car world. In a way, it harked back to the sport's early days, when hot-rodders first began souping up everyday vehicles in their backyards.

The man most associated with this phenomenon was Bob Glidden. He and his

Pro Stock pioneer Bob Glidden gets off the line at the 1984 NHRA Summernationals. The Pro Stock class exploded in popularity during the 1980s.

1985, Garlits became the first driver to win six Top Fuel events in a season. Other noteworthy performers in the category were Darrell Gwynn and Gary Ormsby, who matched Big Daddy's six wins in 1988 and 1989, respectively. With sponsorship money pouring into the drag racing, competition became particularly fierce during the decade. The sport's rising star was Joe Amato, who won national titles in 1984 and 1988, and went on to dominate the Top Fuel category in the early 1990s.

wife, Etta, considered themselves "weekend warriors" back in the early 1970s. Their interest in the sport was limited by the time they could find to devote to it. But then they entered a big meet in 1972 and Bob shocked the rest of the field by advancing all the way to the finals. Needless to say, this turn of events got the Gliddens more involved in racing. By the time the Pro Stock category began to take off a decade later, the Glidden family—including sons Billy and Rusty—were its dominant force. "Bad Bob" won the NHRA championship in 1980, and again each year from 1985 to 1989. His string was broken by his main nemesis, Bob Shepherd, who took the NHRA Pro Stock title each year from 1981 to 1984. Glidden continued racing stock cars right into the 1990s, winning 85 major titles and claiming 10 championships.

Meanwhile, Don Garlits kept right on going, and his Top Fuel duels with Shirley Muldowney pushed him to new heights. In

Don Garlits, who was still going strong in the 1980s. In 1985, "Big Daddy" became the first driver to win six major Top Fuel events in the same season.

Grand Prix Racing: The 1990s

The moody, stubborn, and often childish behavior of Ayrton Senna would have gotten him kicked off of most teams had he been racing in an earlier era. But as the 1990s began, his genius behind the wheel overshadowed all of his personal shortcomings. Grand Prix racing was a phenomenally expensive enterprise, and if you had a winning driver, you did whatever you could to keep him happy. For McLaren, this meant acceding to Senna's wishes and allowing Alain Prost to leave for arch rival Ferrari, where he joined Nigel Mansell until Mansell decided to move on.

To its credit, FISA did try to control Senna. He was fined for his reckless driving and skirting of the rules, and his 1989 World Championship was taken away. But these moves had eye-opening consequences, FISA president Jean-Marie Balestre had to hire bodyguards to protect him from Senna's furious fans in 1990. For the first time, the powers in auto racing were wondering whether a day might come when drivers were actually bigger than their sport.

Otherwise, the 1990 season proceeded as expected, with the competition between Senna and Prost more cutthroat than ever, and Mansell applying constant pressure all year long. In the final race, with Senna a few points ahead of Prost, they went into the first corner side by side, with neither man willing to give way. In a replay of 1989, the cars slammed together and spun into the sand, giving Senna the driver's championship. In 1991, there was far less drama. Senna's car suffered from frequent computer malfunctions—when it worked, he won. Prost's Ferrari, on the other hand, was not terribly competitive. Mansell, who had left Ferrari for Williams, put the most heat on Senna, winning the French, British, German, Italian, and Spanish Grand Prixes. But in the end Senna's immense talent prevailed, as he finished the year strong to win his third World Championship.

Mansell finally managed to break through in 1992, behind the wheel of the new Williams FW14B, which had a little more power than Senna's McLaren. Mansell, who had once threatened to retire, became the only driver ever to win the first five events of a Grand Prix season. When Senna took a couple of races, the Englishman responded by reeling off wins in France, Britain, Germany, and Portugal. Not only did Mansell squash Senna, he beat the Brazilian's record of eight wins in a season.

Mansell's big year was also a triumph for team owner Frank Williams, who had lost the use of his arms and legs in a 1986 car accident. Rather than retiring, Williams returned to the garage, where he supervised creation of the FW14B. This amazing car had computer-activated suspension, which allowed it to adjust automatically to achieve the optimum aerodynamics and weight distribution on any corner at any speed.

After his remarkable year, Mansell surprised the Formula One establishment by moving to the Indy car circuit. Infuriated at McLaren for what he believed to be an inferior car, Senna offered to drive for Williams in 1993 for free! Much to Senna's chagrin, Williams opted for his old nemesis, Alain Prost, who had spent the previous season in retirement. Prost teamed with rookie Damon Hill (son of the great Graham Hill) to keep Williams on top all year long. Prost

THE BEST EVER?

In an age when competing in Formula One is more like landing a jet than driving the family car, Ayrton Senna reminded fans of the links to the sport's glorious past. He drove with passion, bravado, and daring. He intimidated competitors by running qualifying laps at reckless speeds, and grabbed more pole positions than anyone in history. Senna would pass anytime, anywhere, and took great delight in doing so at the most dangerous spots on the course. Senna's rivalry with Alain Prost was particularly engrossing because Prost approached his profession from an entirely different point of view. He was a perfectionist who never took chances, the ultimate textbook racer. Senna was supremely confident—more so perhaps than anyone since Tazio Nuvolari. He asked for $1 million a race and he got it. He demanded to be treated like a god, and he was. Other drivers called him the best ever. Historians were inclined to agree.

won his fourth world title with seven victories, while Hill took three races late in the season.

The 1994 Grand Prix season opened with great promise. Prost retired for good, leaving a high-paying opening at Williams, which Senna was all too happy to fill. The thought of Senna—the sport's superstar—behind the wheel of the sport's supercar was very exciting, especially with rising stars Damon Hill and Michael Schumacher on his tail. But tragedy struck at San Marino, when Austria's Roland Ratzenberger was killed during practice. His death shook the Formula One world, which had not had a driving fatality since 1982. Indeed, Grand Prix fans merely assumed that, thanks to advances in safety, a driver could walk away from any crash, regardless of its severity. Two days later, the unfathomable occurred when Senna, who was leading the race, skidded off the road and slammed head-on into a barrier at 185 mph. He was killed instantly. A month later, another top driver, Karl Wendlinger, cracked up at Monaco and needed a miracle recovery to avoid becoming the third fatality of the season.

This left the way clear for Schumacher and Hill, who went down to the wire in 1994 before Schumacher, driving for Team Benetton, edged Hill for the championship by a single point. Recalling the feud between Prost and Senna, Schumacher and Hill began sniping at each other from the beginning of the year, with Schumacher claiming Hill was dumb, and Hill characterizing Schumacher as dangerously selfish. Hill experienced this firsthand, when he attempted to pass his rival in the season's last event only to have Schumacher bash into him.

Schumacher hogged the glory again in 1995. In fact, he ran away with the driver's

Michael Schumacher and Jacques Villeneuve share a 1997 cover of *Racer* magazine. In the absence of Ayrton Senna, their rivalry became the big story in Formula One.

title, scoring a record nine victories to earn a place in the history books. The German star also earned one of the most lucrative deals in the history of sports, signing a two-year contract to drive for Ferrari for $48 million. Seeing Schumacher rake in so much money, Indy car superstar Jacques Villeneuve (the son of Gilles Villeneuve) decided to follow in his father's footsteps and join the Formula One circuit in 1996. In an off-season that saw almost every major driver change teams, Villeneuve signed on to replace Schumacher at Williams, where he would get a great car and a great teammate in Hill. It took several months for Schumacher to get comfortable in his new Ferrari, and during that time Hill captured seven races to sew up the driving title. To the great delight of Williams, Villeneuve took 4 events during the same period, giving Williams a remarkable 11 victories in the season's first 13 races. Hill finished the

year with his eighth victory to win his first World Championship.

In 1997, Schumacher righted himself and finished first or second a total of eight times going into the season's final race. But Villeneuve was just as good, scoring seven victories to come within a point of the German. At the European Grand Prix, Schumacher was in the lead with Villeneuve coming up fast in second place. As Villeneuve attempted to pass him on the 48th lap, Schumacher tried the same trick he had used to win the championship in 1994, when he banged into Hill. But Villeneuve, a veteran of the rough-and-tumble CART races, held firm, causing Schumacher to bounce the other way, off the track and out of the race. As they say, what goes around comes around. While Schumacher tried unsuccessfully to get his car back in order, Villeneuve wobbled to a third-place finish, which was enough to win the 1997 driving championship.

Indy-Car Racing: The 1990s

The 1990 Indianapolis 500 saw its second overseas winner in a row, with Holland's Arie Luyendyk taking the checkered flag. It also marked the third consecutive victory for the special Chevrolet Indy V-8 engine introduced to the race by Roger Penske in 1986. With the top six finishers all sporting this engine, it put the final nail in the coffin of Cosworth, which by now had shifted its focus back to Grand Prix cars. Cosworth took some consolation from the fact that Indy's new engine of choice was manufactured in England by Mario Ilien and Paul Morgan, both of whom were former Cosworth engineers.

Penske star Rick Mears won the race in 1991, making him only the second driver to take the checkered flag at Indy in three different decades. And Al Unser, Jr., won in 1992 to erase any ill will left over from the tag-team tactics he employed to help his fa-

ther back in 1983. The 1992 Indianapolis 500 was truly a family affair. Both Unsers were in the race, as was Mario Andretti, along with his sons, Jeff and Michael, and his nephew, John. It was a thrilling race, with many crashes, plenty of passing, and a photo finish, as Al Jr. crossed the finish line four one hundredths of a second ahead of Canadian Scott Goodyear. Emerson Fittipaldi, the 1989 winner, won again in 1993. This race was notable for the absences of Indy fixtures A. J. Foyt and Mears, as well as the appearance of Formula One legend Nigel Mansell, who impressed everyone by finishing third. Veteran Gary Bettenhausen made the starting field, meaning that (along with Andretti and Unser) there were three grandfathers in the race. It would be the last 500 for Andretti and Unser, who retired soon after.

Fittipaldi looked like a good bet to win again in 1994, thanks to Penske, who detected a loophole in the race's new engine specifications. Taking full advantage of this

Al Unser, Jr., holds off hard-charging Scott Goodyear to win the 1992 Indy 500 by a fraction of a second.

opportunity, he had special Mercedes engines modified just for the 500, and entered Fittipaldi and his newest driver, Al Unser, Jr. The two dominated the race, with Emmo building a comfortable lead in the late going. But with just a few laps to go, Fittipaldi inexplicably attempted to lap Unser. He clipped the wall and spun out, allowing his teammate to win. Fans who witnessed Fittipaldi's 1989 victory smiled at the irony of the crash. They remembered that it was he who had sent Unser into the wall in that race, as they were dueling for the lead with less than two laps to go.

Just when it looked as if the 1990s would belong to Roger Penske, the oddest thing happened: not one of his cars qualified for the 1995 Indianapolis 500. That left the field wide open, and also set the tone for a bizarre finish. Scott Goodyear, driving the race of his life, passed the pace car during a caution period and was penalized with just a few laps to go. His countryman, Jacques Villeneuve, who was not considered one of the favorites in the race, won it instead. In second place was Fittipaldi—not Emerson but his nephew, Christian, who was driving at Indy for the first time.

Things got even weirder in 1996, when Indy-car racing literally tore itself apart. Prior to the 1996 season, Tony George, president of the Indianapolis Motor Speedway, announced the launch of a new association, the Indy Racing League. The announcement, in and of itself, was not earth-shattering news to CART officials. The fledgling IRL had only three races on its schedule, and CART still had all the top drivers. But then the IRL changed the qualifying rules for the Indy 500, and the fireworks started.

To attract teams and drivers to the new league, George announced that 25 of the 33 qualifying spots for the 1996 race would be reserved for IRL cars. The leaders of CART were furious. Claiming they were being locked out of the most high-profile event on the racing schedule, they maintained that CART teams, drivers, and sponsors stood to lose millions of dollars. On both counts, they were absolutely correct.

From its humble beginnings in the 1970s, CART had developed into one of the most successful leagues in auto-racing history. Its schedule by this time included 16 races at beautiful venues around the world, including the United States, Canada, Australia, and Brazil. The circuit had also become tremendously lucrative, with drivers earning millions each year. TV ratings soared. CART races were televised in more than 150 nations, and more than 50 million people in the U.S. tuned into CART events each year. Needless to say, there was a lot at stake, especially if only a handful of CART drivers were able to compete at Indy.

The Indy Racing League is announced, touching off a feud with CART that would tear U.S. racing apart.

So for 1996, the real action was not on the track, but in the courtroom, as each side acted to protect its own interests. CART struck the most powerful blow when it scheduled the "U.S. 500" to be held on the same day as the Indianapolis 500. The plan was to sink Indy by withholding all of the sport's top racers. Undaunted, IRL moved forward, refusing to budge.

The big losers in this battle, of course, were the fans. They had supported Indy racing in record numbers, and their "reward" had always been the Indy 500. Yet now they were being forced to choose between watching a big race run by a bunch of no-names, and a no-name race with all of the stars. They were already smarting from the loss of the flashy young Villeneuve—CART's 1994 Rookie of the Year and the winner of the 1995 Indy 500—who had departed to drive Formula One. By the time May 1996 rolled around, there was only lukewarm support for the Indy 500, while the U.S. 500 was totally ignored.

Realizing their folly, CART and IRL forged an uneasy peace for the 1997 season. They continued to run competing racing circuits, but IRL agreed to return to the old qualifying rules at the Indianapolis 500 and CART promised not to run a competing race. The fans got what they wanted, with more top-level racing than ever. They could watch IRL events and root for the likes of Eddie Cheever, Scott Goodyear, Roberto Guerrero, and Arie Luyendyk (who won the 1997 500). Or they could tune into CART races and watch Jimmy Vasser, Michael Andretti, Alex Zanardi, and Al Unser, Jr., go for the checkered flag. Best of all, all the top drivers were allowed to go to the Brickyard and pursue the biggest prize in their sport. As the 21st century neared, the fate of

Indy racing was unclear. But at least a total disaster had been avoided.

NASCAR Racing: The 1990s

The big beneficiary of the struggle in Indy-car racing was NASCAR, which enjoyed another record-shattering season. Not that stock-car racing needed any help. During the first half of the 1990s, NASCAR's television ratings climbed steadily, while attendance at Winston Cup events practically tripled. From its roots as a backwoods pastime, it had become a bona fide mainstream American sport, with fans in every region of the country. And during the 1990s NASCAR races moved into some of the largest metropolitan markets in the U.S., including Indianapolis, Dallas/Fort Worth, and Los Angeles. In 1996, a demonstration race was even run in Suzuka, Japan. Even though stock-car racing had become incredibly sophisticated (by the end of the 1980s, cars contained virtually no factory parts) and millions of dollars were at stake in each race, NASCAR still retained its down-home appeal and continued to build on its own mythology.

The high drama was supplied by Jeff Gordon, the soft-spoken new kid in town, and Dale Earnhardt, the grizzled old gunslinger. Earnhardt—loved by some, reviled by others—surged to the top of the Winston Cup standings with his give-no-ground, take-no-prisoners approach. He was NASCAR champ in 1990, 1991, 1993, and 1994, putting together the most impressive run by a driver since the glory days of Richard Petty. In 1997, he surpassed the $30-million mark in career earnings—the most of any driver in any kind of motor

Dale Earnhardt surges past Jeff Gordon to take command of the 1998 Daytona 500, writing a dramatic new chapter in their rivalry.

exhibited, and certainly no one his age had ever been so advanced. Gordon finished first, second, or third in 13 races in 1995 to win the Winston Cup title at the tender age of 24. Right on his tail that year—both literally and figuratively—was Earnhardt, who missed his third consecutive championship by a scant 34 points. Gordon took 10 events in 1996 and again in 1997, winning the 1997 NASCAR title. Understandably, his was the face most of stock-car racing's new fans most associated with the sport.

While the 1990s brought unprecedented growth to NASCAR, it also brought unspeakable tragedy. Bobby Allison's son,

sport—and became a car owner himself in 1998. As more and more young drivers entered the sport, Earnhardt came to represent NASCAR's "old school." On his official bio, he listed his favorite food as steak and his favorite movie as *The Outlaw Josey Wales.* He once described his driving style as "Rubbin' Racin'"—which is another way of saying that, to Earnhardt's way of thinking, there is nothing wrong with a little "incidental" contact, even at 200 mph.

Gordon, of course, was part of racing's new wave. In a sport where drivers typically work their way up a long and grueling ladder before getting a NASCAR ride, he was a genuine prodigy. At the age of 6, Gordon was beating teenagers in Go-Kart events; by 12 he was outracing adults on the quarter-midget circuit. And by his 21st birthday Gordon was one of the top drivers in the world. Few, if any, had the kind of feel for a car he

Dale Earnhardt celebrates his first Daytona 500 win, in 1998. The victory came in his 20th attempt, breaking NASCAR's most famous "jinx."

Davey, had become a fan favorite after winning his first race back in 1987. He lived in Alabama and called the Talladega Speedway his home track. Ironically, it was there that Allison met with disaster, when his helicopter crashed in the infield. Just 11 months after his younger brother Cliff had died in a practice crash, Davey Allison was dead. More than 100,000 people attended his memorial, during which Uncle Donnie drove his nephew's car—number 28—around the track one last time.

Allison's death rocked the racing world, which was already reeling from the loss of another beloved driver that spring. Alan Kulwicki, the 1992 Winston Cup champion, died when an airplane carrying him and three others crashed on the way to a race in Bristol, Tennessee. Like Gordon, Kulwicki was one of racing's new breed. He was born in Wisconsin (which made him the first NASCAR champ from north of the Mason-Dixon line) and held a college degree. Rather than looking for a sponsor, Kulwicki preferred to scrape along on his own, preferring to run his team his way. NASCAR also lost veteran Neil Bonnett during the 1990s, when he crashed during qualifying for the 1994 Daytona 500 and died from massive head injuries.

For all of the sadness the 1990s brought to NASCAR, it was also a time for celebration. Competition was fierce, and several talented drivers broke through during this period. Besides Gordon and Kulwicki, the other drivers to emerge during the decade were Mark Martin, Ernie Irvan, Jeff Burton, Sterling Marlin, Dale Jarrett, and Bobby Labonte. Martin won his first race in 1989 and finished third among NASCAR drivers, then remained at or near the top of the rankings throughout the 1990s. A walking con-

tradition, he could wolf down junk food with any NASCAR fan, yet spent countless hours in the gym working on his strength and conditioning. Irvan won his first race in 1990 and took the Daytona 500 in 1991. He seemed headed toward greatness when a 1994 crash kept him off the track for a year. Doctors originally gave Irvan a 1 in 10 chance of surviving his injuries, but by 1996 he was back in the winner's circle. Burton reached the winner's circle for the first time in 1997, which was just his fourth full year on the Winston Cup circuit. The younger brother of veteran Ward Burton, he finished more than a quarter of his 1997 starts first, second, or third, and finished fourth overall in the standings to cap off a spectacular breakthrough season.

Marlin—whose father "Coo Coo" entered more than 300 NASCAR races from 1970 to 1980 without a single winning one—had 279 starts himself before winning his first event in 1994. That race happened to be the Daytona 500, and this feat was hailed as one of the great flukes in sports history. But one year later Marlin won his second career race: the Daytona 500 again! Overnight he went from being a lovable loser to one of the most respected drivers on the circuit. Jarrett also followed in his father's footsteps, winning the Daytona 500 in 1993 and 1996, and capturing seven races in 1997 to finish just behind Jeff Gordon in the year-end standings. A tremendously focused and precise driver, Jarrett passed the $10-million mark in career earnings—a figure some claim he could also have topped had he chosen to go into professional golf. Labonte, whose older brother Terry became NASCAR champ for the second time in 1996, cracked the Top 10 in 1995 and again in 1997. As for Terry, he led a group of old favorites like Bill

Elliott, Rusty Wallace, and Ricky Rudd (who won at least one NASCAR event 15 years in a row) that continued to put up strong seasons throughout the 1990s.

As stock-car racing approached the 21st century, it was in spectacular shape. Its public-relations and marketing people had become nearly as sophisticated as its mechanics and engineers, ensuring a steady stream of media coverage and income as the sport continued to expand into every part of the United States. NASCAR's strength was no more evident than when the government announced its plans to ban all outdoor tobacco advertising. A decade earlier this might have crippled the sport, which had relied heavily on its corporate ties with Winston since the early 1970s. But during the 1990s the trend toward more mainstream consumer sponsors had steadily picked up momentum, and the loss of Winston money did not seem to phase NASCAR officials one bit. If anything, the move away from tobacco sponsorship made stock-car racing even more appealing to potential sponsors as America's ultimate "family" sport.

Drag Racing: The 1990s

On March 20, 1992, Kenny Bernstein tore down a quarter-mile track in Gainesville, Florida at the eye-popping speed of 301.7 miles per hour. It marked the first time a Top Fuel dragster had ever reached that speed, and it came 17 years after Don Garlits first cracked the 250-mph barrier. By the end of the 1990s, speeds on the drag strip would regularly top 315 miles per hour, and fans began talking about what it would take to reach 350.

Kenny Bernstein is little more than a blur as he blows away the field at the 1992 Winternationals in California. That same season, Bernstein cracked the 300-mph barrier—17 years after Don Garlits reached the 250-mph plateau.

The Top Fuel category saw veterans Bernstein and Joe Amato deal with a group of new challengers, including Cory McClenathan, Scott Kalitta, and Gary Scelzi. The new force in Funny Cars during the 1990s was John Force, who obliterated the career victories mark set by Don Prudhomme and dominated his class throughout the decade. Funny cars joined the triple-century club in 1993, when Jim Epler cracked the 300-mph barrier. The Pro Stock category remained hot, with Bob Glidden yielding his crown to new stars Darrell Alderman and Warren Johnson, who surpassed the 200-mph mark in April 1997.

With increased speed, however, came increased risk. As was the case in Formula One, it had been a long time since death had taken a top driver. In fact, not since the mid-1970s had there been a fatality during an NHRA Top Fuel national event. But in 1996 Blaine Johnson—a popular 34-year-old driver on the circuit—met his demise in a violent crash. The tragedy impacted everyone in drag racing, especially because Johnson had been so well liked. He was known both as a fearless competitor and a class act. His death not only left a void in the upper ranks of the Top Fuel standings, but caused many of his fellow drivers to reassess, at least temporarily, their place in the sport.

Of course, as in any of the motor sports, the fear of death lingers in the back of the minds of all drag racers. In heats that rarely last more than five seconds, it comes quickly and with no warning. As much as drivers hate to admit it, once they "light the candle" there is nothing they can do if something goes wrong.

Despite Johnson's death, the popularity of drag racing grew steadily throughout the 1990s, attracting enough sponsorship

Blaine Johnson, the first fatality in two decades at an NHRA Top Fuel event, caused many in drag racing to wonder, "How fast is too fast?"

money to keep engine technology at the cutting edge. Like NASCAR, a lot of new corporate sponsorships were formed with more mainstream, family-oriented advertisers, broadening the sport's financial base beyond automotive companies. Still, drag racing was very dependent on tobacco money, as Winston had been the NHRA's chief sponsor for many years. With the changes in laws governing this type of advertising, the short-term effects on the sport's health heading into the 21st century were unclear.

What was clear is that the next century should bring to drag racing tremendous excitement and unprecedented achievement. The insatiable thirst for speed and the fundamental appeal of one-on-one competition gives the sport a unique pull on the human psyche, and creates a bond between driver and fan that is every bit as strong as that which exists between the athletes and spectators in any other form of racing.

Speeding Into a New Millenium

Those who understand how far racing has come since Count Jules de Dion was the only entrant in history's first auto race also marvel at how little in the sport actually has changed. The people who design and build cars are searching for the same relationships between power, weight, balance, and reliability. The people who drive cars are still trying to achieve that perfect union between man and machine. And the people who cheer their favorites to victory still go for the speed, the danger, and the sweet perfume of burning rubber, high-powered fuel, and engine exhaust. Where racing is headed as it enters its third century is difficult to say. The forces of friction and gravity—and the laws of physics—conspire to limit how fast a car can propel itself over a stretch of road. There are, however, emerging factors that might blur those boundaries. What, for instance, will be the effect on racing as computing speed grows expo-

nentially, and as computers find their way deeper into the driver-vehicle relationship? How might new car-building and track-building materials change the way races are run? And as humankind reaches for new energy sources, is it even safe to assume that cars will be powered by gasoline a few decades from now? Perhaps the most significant changes will come in the form of "new" drivers. There is a generation of kids out there who traded their wooden go-karts for video games. Their hand-eye coordination and fine motor control is incredible, and they have "died" so many times in their games that they have no fear of failure. A few will no doubt venture into motor sports, and they will be perfectly comfortable pushing buttons and toggling joysticks, if that is what it takes to win races in the 21st century. Who knows? Over the next 100 years, steering, shifting, and braking may be hands-free, with commands coming directly from the driver's mind! Indeed, auto racing could be a dramatically different business than it is today.

An Auto Racing Timeline

1863 The first gas-fueled motor car is demonstrated by Etienne Lenoir in Paris.

1887 The first race for motor cars, sponsored by *Le Velocipede,* is won by Count Jules de Dion, the only entrant.

1894 The first long-distance road race (Paris-to-Rouen) is held.

1895 Edouard Michelin becomes the first racer to use pneumatic tires; the world's first motoring organizations—the American Motor League (Chicago) and Auto Club de France (Paris)—are formed.

1899 Madame Labrousse becomes the first woman to participate in an automobile race (Paris-to-Spain); the Automobile Club of America is formed.

1900 The first race exclusively for female drivers is held outside of London; the first Gordon Bennett Trophy race is held in France.

1901 Camille du Gast becomes the unofficial queen of auto racing when she finishes 33rd in the Paris-to-Berlin race.

1902 The American Automobile Association is formed; Barney

Oldfield wins his first major race, in Michigan.

1903 Oldfield becomes the first driver to cover a mile in under a minute on a circular track.

1904 Louis Rigolly, driving a Gobron-Brillie, becomes the first driver to exceed 100 mph; the first "mass-produced" car is marketed by Oldsmobile ($650); the first Vanderbilt Cup race is held on Long Island.

1905 The first 24-hour race is held in France.

1906 The first Targa Florio race is held in Italy.

1907 The world's first racing course is built in Brooklands, south of London.

1908 George Robertson becomes the first American driver to win the Vanderbilt Cup race.

1911 The first 500-mile race is held at Indianapolis. Ray Harroun is the winner.

1914 Four-wheel brakes are introduced to Grand Prix racing.

1920 Jimmy Murphy moves the land speed record over the 150-mph mark in a Duesenberg.

1921 Motorcycle racer Tazio Nuvolari enters his first auto race in Italy and finishes third.

1922 The Monza Autodrome opens in Italy.

1924 American superstars Jimmy Murphy and Joe Boyer are killed in separate board speedway accidents; Dario Resta burns to death after a crash at Brooklands.

1927 World War I ace Eddie Rickenbacker purchases the Indianapolis Motor Speedway from Carl Fisher; Germany's Nurburgring officially opens; Henry Segrave, in a Sunbeam Slug, becomes the first driver to break the 200-mph barrier; Grand Prix entrants are allowed to drive solo for the first time; the Mille Miglia is held for the first time in the mountains of northern Italy.

1928 Fritz von Opel goes from 0 to 60 mph in under 8 seconds in a rocket-powered car.

1929 The legendary road circuit in Monaco is opened; Indy 500 winner Ray Keech dies in an accident on America's last operating board speedway; Cannonball Baker drives a Franklin from Los Angeles to New York in 2 days, 21 1/2 hours.

1930 Alfa Romeo's Enzo Ferrari starts his own racing team.

1932 Ferdinand Porsche forms his own company.

1935 Sir Malcolm Campbell breaks the 300-mph barrier in his Bluebird at the Bonneville Salt Flats in Utah.

1938 Alfa Romeo's legendary Alfetta 158 finishes first and second in its debut race; John Cobb, in a Railton Special, pushes the land speed record over 350 mph.

1941 Louis Unser wins the Pike's Peak hill climb in the last racing event before America enters the war.

1944 The Sports Car Club of America is formed in Boston.

1946 The first race of the postwar era is held on the sand at Daytona Beach, Florida.

1947 Bill France forms NASCAR.

1951 Disc brakes make their racing debut at the Indianapolis 500.

1952 Hermann Lang, Germany's rising star during the 1930s, wins the 24-hour race at Le Mans with Fritz Riess.

1954 Every car starting the Indy 500 uses the same engine, a four-cylinder Offenhauser.

1955 83 spectators are killed in a crash at Le Mans; AAA withdraws from auto racing after the crash. The U.S. Auto Club steps in as the governing body in American racing.

1956 NASCAR team owner Carl Kiekhafer racks up a record 30 wins sponsoring drivers Buck Baker (14), Speedy Thompson (8), Herb Thomas (3), Tim Flock (3), Fonty Flock (1), and Jack Smith (1).

1957 Juan-Manuel Fangio wins his fourth consecutive world driving championship; for the first time, the Indy 500 is started with the famous words, "Gentlemen, start your engines."

1958 Mike Costin and Keith Duckworth form Cosworth Engines; A.J. Foyt wins his first Indy 500; Fireball Roberts wins 60 percent of the stock car races he enters.

1959 The Daytona International Speedway is completed.

1961 The last significant section of exposed brick is paved over at Indianapolis; sweeping safety regulations come to Grand Prix racing, as roll bars, dual braking and ignition cut-out switches are made mandatory in all cars; Phil Hill becomes the first American to win the world championship.

1962 Parnelli Jones becomes the first Indy driver to qualify at over 150 mph; 20-year-old Ricardo Rodriguez, the rising star in Grand Prix racing, is killed during practice.

1964 Prize money at Indy exceeds $500,000 for the first time; Donald Campbell breaks the 400-mph barrier in a jet-powered car. He dies three years later attempting to set the water-speed mark.

1965 Mario Andretti makes his Indy debut, finishing third; NASCAR's Ned Jarrett completes his second straight season with 45 Top 10 finishes.

1967 Richard Petty wins a record 27 NASCAR races.

1969 NASCAR's Bobby Isaac earns the pole position a record 20 times.

1970 Indy prize money climbs above $1 million for the first time; high-traction treadless "slick" tires—long a staple of drag racing—come to Grand Prix racing.

1971 Al Unser becomes the first driver to use a radio to communicate with his pit crew.

1972 Renault returns to racing after an absence of 66 years; A.J. Foyt becomes the first driver to win the Daytona 500, Indy 500, and 24-hour race at Le Mans.

1973 Porsche unveils the 1,100-horsepower Spyder, the most powerful circuit racing car ever built; Jackie Stewart establishes a new record for Grand Prix victories with 28.

1977 Tom Sneva becomes the first driver to exceed 200 mph in Indy qualifying; Janet Guthrie becomes the first woman to qualify for the Indianapolis 500; Shirley Muldowney wins her first NHRA Top Fuel drag racing championship.

1978 CART takes on USAC, running its first series of Indy car races; Cale Yarborough becomes the first NASCAR driver to win three consecutive Winston Cup championships.

1982 The total purse for Indy exceeds $2 million for the first time.

1983 Richard Noble, in his jet-powered Thrust II, breaks the 600-mph barrier.

1984 Richard Petty wins his 200th NASCAR race.

1986 Bill Elliott wins three of NASCAR's "big four" races to earn stock-car racing's first $1-million bonus.

1987 Dale Earnhardt becomes the first NASCAR driver to earn more than $2 million in prize money during a season.

1990 Random drug testing comes to Grand Prix racing.

1992 The world's top Grand Prix driver, Ayrton Senna, dies in a crash; Richard Petty retires after his record 35th year on the NASCAR circuit.

1993 Lyn St. James becomes the second woman to qualify for the Indianapolis 500.

1997 Jeff Gordon wins his 25th NASCAR race in his 137th career start—61 starts faster than the previous record-holder, Darrell Waltrip.

1998 Two-time CART champion Alex Zanardi announces he is leaving to join the Formula One circuit.

APPENDIX A:
Formula One Records

Most Grand Prix Victories

Driver, Country	Victories	Career Poles
Alain Prost, France	51	33
Ayrton Senna, Brazil	41	65
Michael Schumacher, Germany	37	17
Nigel Mansell, Great Britain	31	32
Jackie Stewart, Great Britain	27	17
Jim Clark, Great Britain	25	33
Niki Lauda, Austria	25	24
Juan-Manuel Fangio, Argentina	24	28
Nelson Piquet, Brazil	23	24
Damon Hill, Great Britain	22	20

Formula One World Champions

Year	Driver, Country	Car
1950	Giuseppe Farina, Italy	Alfa Romeo
1951	Juan-Manuel Fangio, Argentina	Alfa Romeo
1952	Alberto Ascari, Italy	Ferrari
1953	Alberto Ascari, Italy	Ferrari
1954	Juan-Manuel Fangio, Argentina	Maserati & Mercedes*
1955	Juan-Manuel Fangio, Argentina	Mercedes
1956	Juan-Manuel Fangio, Argentina	Ferrari
1957	Juan-Manuel Fangio, Argentina	Maserati
1958	Mike Hawthorn, Great Britain	Ferrari
1959	Jack Brabham, Australia	Cooper Climax
1960	Jack Brabham, Australia	Cooper Climax
1961	Phil Hill, United States	Ferrari
1962	Graham Hill, Great Britain	BRM
1963	Jim Clark, Great Britain	Lotus Climax
1964	John Surtees, Great Britain	Ferrari
1965	Jim Clark, Great Britain	Lotus Climax
1966	Jack Brabham, Australia	Brabham Repco
1967	Dennis Hulme, New Zealand	Brabham Repco
1968	Graham Hill, Great Britain	Lotus Ford
1969	Jackie Stewart, Great Britain	Matra Ford
1970	Jochen Rindt, Austria	Lotus Ford
1971	Jackie Stewart, Great Britain	Tyrrell Ford
1972	Emerson Fittipaldi, Brazil	Lotus Ford
1973	Jackie Stewart, Great Britain	Tyrrell Ford
1974	Emerson Fittipaldi, Brazil	McLaren Ford
1975	Niki Lauda, Austria	Ferrari
1976	James Hunt, Great Britain	McLaren Ford
1977	Niki Lauda, Austria	Ferrari
1978	Mario Andretti, United States	Lotus Ford
1979	Jody Scheckter, South Africa	Ferrari
1980	Alan Jones, Australia	Williams Ford
1981	Nelson Piquet, Brazil	Brabham Ford
1982	Keke Rosberg, Finland	Williams Ford
1983	Nelson Piquet, Brazil	Brabham BMW Turbo
1984	Niki Lauda, Austria	McLaren TAG Porsche Turbo
1985	Alain Prost, France	McLaren TAG Porsche Turbo
1986	Alain Prost, France	McLaren TAG Porsche Turbo
1987	Nelson Piquet, Brazil	Williams Honda Turbo
1988	Ayrton Senna, Brazil	McLaren Honda Turbo
1989	Alain Prost, France	McLaren Honda
1990	Ayrton Senna, Brazil	McLaren Honda
1991	Ayrton Senna, Brazil	McLaren Honda
1992	Nigel Mansell, Great Britain	Williams Renault
1993	Alain Prost, France	Williams Renault
1994	Michael Schumacher, Germany	Benetton Ford
1995	Michael Schumacher, Germany	Benetton Renault
1996	Damon Hill, Great Britain	Williams Renault
1997	Jacques Villeneuve	Williams Renault

*Drove two cars during year

APPENDIX B:
INDY CAR RECORDS

Career Indy Car	Victories
A.J. Foyt	67
Mario Andretti	52
Al Unser	39
Michael Andretti	37
Bobby Unser	35
Al Unser, Jr.	31
Rick Mears	29
Johnny Rutherford	27
Rodger Ward	26
Gordon Johncock	25

Indianapolis 500 Winners

Year	Driver	Avg. Speed	Car
1911	Ray Harroun	74.6	Marmon Wasp
1912	Joe Dawson	78.7	National
1913	Jules Goux	75.9	Peugeot
1914	Rene Thomas	82.5	Delage
1915	Ralph DePalma	89.8	Mercedes
1916	Dario Resta	84.0	Peugeot
1917-18	World War I - Not Held		
1919	Howdy Wilcox	88.1	Peugeot
1920	Gaston Chevrolet	88.6	Monroe
1921	Tommy Milton	89.6	Frontenac
1922	Jimmy Murphy	94.5	Murphy Special
1923	Tommy Milton	91.0	HCS Special
1924	L.L. Corum/ Joe Boyer	98.2	Duesenberg Special
1925	Peter DePaolo	101.1	Duesenberg Special
1926	Frank Lockhart	95.9	Miller Special
1927	George Souders	97.5	Simplex Piston Ring Special
1928	Louie Meyer	99.5	Miller Special
1929	Ray Keech	97.6	Simplex Piston Ring Special
1930	Billy Arnold	100.4	Miller-Hartz Special
1931	Louis Schneider	96.6	Bowes Seal Fast Special
1932	Fred Frame	104.1	Miller-Hartz Special
1933	Louie Meyer	104.2	Tydol Special
1934	Bill Cummings	104.9	Boyle Products Special
1935	Kelly Petillo	106.2	Gilmore Speedway Special
1936	Louie Meyer	109.1	Ring Free Special
1937	Wilbur Shaw	113.6	Shaw-Gilmore Special
1938	Floyd Roberts	117.2	Burd Piston Ring Special
1939	Wilbur Shaw	115.0	Boyle Special
1940	Wilbur Shaw	114.3	Boyle Special
1941	Floyd Davis/ Mauri Rose	115.1	Noc-Out Hose Clamp Special
1942-45	World War II - Not Held		
1946	George Robson	114.8	Thorne Engineering Special
1947	Mauri Rose	116.3	Blue Crown Spark Plug Special
1948	Mauri Rose	119.8	Blue Crown Spark Plug Special
1949	Bill Holland	121.3	Blue Crown Spark Plug Special
1950	Johnny Parsons	124.0	Wynn's Friction Proofing
1951	Lee Wallard	126.2	Belanger Special
1952	Troy Ruttman	128.9	Agajanian Special
1953	Bill Vukovich	128.7	Fuel injection Special
1954	Bill Vukovich	130.8	Fuel injection Special
1955	Bob Sweikert	128.2	John Zink Special
1956	Pat Flaherty	128.5	John Zink Special
1957	Sam Hanks	135.6	Belond Exhaust Special
1958	Jimmy Bryan	133.8	Belond AP Parts Special
1959	Rodger Ward	135.9	Leader Car 500 Roadster
1960	Jim Rathmann	138.8	Ken-Paul Special
1961	A.J. Foyt	147.4	Bowes Seal Fast Special

Year	Driver	Speed	Car
1962	Rodger Ward	140.3	Leader Car 500 Roadster
1963	Parnelli Jones	143.1	Agajanian-Willard Special
1964	A.J. Foyt	147.4	Sheraton-Thompson Special
1965	Jim Clark	150.7	Lotus Ford
1966	Graham Hill	144.3	American Red Ball Special
1967	A.J. Foyt	151.2	Sheraton-Thompson Special
1968	Bobby Unser	152.9	Rislone Special
1969	Mario Andretti	156.9	STP Special
1970	Al Unser	155.7	Johnny Lightning Special
1971	Al Unser	157.7	Johnny Lightning Special
1972	Mark Donohue	163.0	Sunoco McLaren
1973	Gordon Johncock	159.0	STP Special
1974	Johnny Rutherford	158.6	McLaren
1975	Bobby Unser	149.2	Jorgensen Eagle
1976	Johnny Rutherford	148.7	Hy-Gain McLaren Goodyear
1977	A.J. Foyt	161.3	Gilmore Racing Team
1978	Al Unser	161.3	Chaparral Lola
1979	Rick Mears	158.9	Gould Charge
1980	Johnny Rutherford	142.9	Pennzoil Chaparral
1981	Bobby Unser	139.1	Norton Spirit Penske PC-9B
1982	Gordon Johncock	162.0	STP Special
1983	Tom Sneva	162.1	Texaco Star
1984	Rick Mears	163.6	Pennzoil Z-7
1985	Danny Sullivan	153.0	Miller American Special
1986	Bobby Rahal	170.7	Budweiser Truesports March
1987	Al Unser	162.2	Cummins Holset Turbo
1988	Rick Mears	144.8	Pennzoil Z-7 Penske Chevy V-8
1989	Emerson Fittipaldi	167.6	Marlboro Penske Chevy V-8
1990	Arie Luyendyk	186.0	Domino's Pizza Chevrolet
1991	Rick Mears	176.5	Marlboro Penske Chevy
1992	Al Unser, Jr.	160.9	Valvoline Galmer
1993	Emerson Fittipaldi	157.2	Marlboro Penske Chevy
1994	Al Unser, Jr.	160.9	Marlboro Penske Mercedes
1995	Jacques Villeneuve	153.6	Players Ltd. Reynard Ford
1996	Buddy Lazier	148.0	Reynard Ford
1997	Arie Luyendyk	145.8	G-Force Olds Aurora
1998	Eddie Cheever	145.2	Dallara Aurora

APPENDIX C:
STOCK-CAR RACING RECORDS

Career	Victories
Richard Petty	200
David Pearson	105
Bobby Allison	85
Darrell Waltrip	84
Cale Yarborough	83
Dale Earnhardt	71
Lee Petty	54
Ned Jarrett	50
Junior Johnson	50
Herb Thomas	48

Wins in a Season/Driver		
Richard Petty	1967	27
Richard Petty	1971	21
Tim Flock	1955	18
Richard Petty	1970	18
Bobby Isaac	1969	17
David Pearson	1968	16
Richard Petty	1968	16
Ned Jarrett	1964	15
David Pearson	1966	15

NASCAR Champions

Year	Overall Champion	Most Wins
1949	Red Byron	Red Byron & Bob Flock (2)
1950	Bill Rexford	Curtis Tuner (4)
1951	Herb Thomas	Fonty Flock (8)
1952	Tim Flock	Tim Flock & Herb Thomas (8)
1953	Herb Thomas	Herb Thomas (12)
1954	Lee Petty	Herb Thomas (12)
1955	Tim Flock	Tim Flock (18)
1956	Buck Baker	Buck Baker (14)
1957	Buck Baker	Buck Baker (10)
1958	Lee Petty	Lee Petty (7)
1959	Lee Petty	Lee Petty (11)
1960	Rex White	Rex White (6)
1961	Ned Jarrett	Joe Weatherly (9)
1962	Joe Weatherly	Joe Weatherly (9)
1963	Joe Weatherly	Richard Petty (14)
1964	Richard Petty	Ned Jarrett (15)
1965	Ned Jarrett	Ned Jarrett & Junior Johnson (13)
1966	David Pearson	David Pearson (15)
1967	Richard Petty	Richard Petty (27)
1968	David Pearson	David Pearson & Richard Petty (16)
1969	David Pearson	Bobby Isaac (17)
1970	Bobby Isaac	Richard Petty (18)
1971	Richard Petty	Richard Petty (21)
1972	Richard Petty	Bobby Allison (10)
1973	Benny Parsons	David Pearson (11)
1974	Richard Petty	Richard Petty & Cale Yarborough (10)
1975	Richard Petty	Richard Petty (13)
1976	Cale Yarborough	David Pearson (10)
1977	Cale Yarborough	Cale Yarborough (9)
1978	Cale Yarborough	Cale Yarborough (10)
1979	Richard Petty	Darrell Waltrip (7)
1980	Dale Earnhardt	Cale Yarborough (6)
1981	Darrell Waltrip	Darrell Waltrip (12)
1982	Darrell Waltrip	Darrell Waltrip (12)
1983	Bobby Allison	Bobby Allison & Darrell Waltrip (6)
1984	Terry Labonte	Darrell Waltrip (7)
1985	Darrell Waltrip	Bill Elliott (11)
1986	Dale Earnhardt	Tim Richmond (7)
1987	Dale Earnhardt	Dale Earnhardt (11)
1988	Bill Elliott	Bill Elliott & Rusty Wallace (6)
1989	Rusty Wallace	Rusty Wallace & Darrell Waltrip (6)
1990	Dale Earnhardt	Dale Earnhardt (9)
1991	Dale Earnhardt	Davey Allison & Harry Gant (5)
1992	Alan Kulwicki	Bill Elliott & Davey Allison (5)
1993	Dale Earnhardt	Rusty Wallace (10)
1994	Dale Earnhardt	Rusty Wallace (8)
1995	Jeff Gordon	Jeff Gordon (7)
1996	Terry Labonte	Jeff Gordon (10)
1997	Jeff Gordon	Jeff Gordon (10)

APPENDIX D:
DRAG RACING RECORDS

NHRA Champions

Top Fuel

1975	Don Garlits
1976	Richard Tharp
1977	Shirley Muldowney
1978	Kelly Brown
1979	Rob Bruins
1980	Shirley Muldowney
1981	Jeb Allen
1982	Shirley Muldowney
1983	Gary Beck
1984	Joe Amato
1985	Don Garlits
1986	Don Garlits
1987	Dick LaHaie
1988	Joe Amato
1989	Gary Ormsby
1990	Joe Amato
1991	Joe Amato
1992	Joe Amato
1993	Eddie Hill
1994	Scott Kalitta
1995	Scott Kalitta
1996	Kenny Bernstein
1997	Gary Scelzi
1998	Joe Amato

Funny Car

1975	Don Prudhomme
1976	Don Prudhomme
1977	Don Prudhomme
1978	Don Prudhomme
1979	Raymond Beadle
1980	Raymond Beadle
1981	Raymond Beadle
1982	Frank Hawley
1983	Frank Hawley
1984	Mark Oswald
1985	Kenny Bernstein
1986	Kenny Bernstein

1987	Kenny Bernstein	1997	John Force	1981	Lee Shepherd	1991	Darrell Alderman
1988	Kenny Bernstein	1998	Al Hoffman	1982	Lee Shepherd	1992	Warren Johnson
1989	Bruce Larson			1983	Lee Shepherd	1993	Warren Johnson
1990	John Force		**Pro Stock**	1984	Lee Shepherd	1994	Darrell Alderman
1991	John Force	1975	Bob Glidden	1985	Bob Glidden	1995	Warren Johnson
1992	Cruz Pedregon	1976	Larry Lombardo	1986	Bob Glidden	1996	Jim Yates
1993	John Force	1977	Don Nicholson	1987	Bob Glidden	1997	Jim Yates
1994	John Force	1978	Bob Glidden	1988	Bob Glidden	1998	Warren Johnson
1995	John Force	1979	Bob Glidden	1989	Bob Glidden		
1996	John Force	1980	Bob Glidden	1990	John Myers		

APPENDIX E:
INTERNATIONAL MOTORSPORTS HALL OF FAME

Drivers

Bobby Allison
Alberto Ascari
Buck Baker
Buddy Baker
Tony Bettenhausen
George Bignotti
Jack Brabham
Malcolm Campbell
Colin Chapman
Louis Chevrolet
Jim Clark
Ralph DePalma
Mark Donohue
Ralph Earnhardt
Richie Evans
Juan-Manuel Fangio

Enzo Ferrari
Tim Flock
Henry Ford
Bill France
Don Garlits
Andy Granatelli
Peter Gregg
Dan Gurney
Donald Haley
Jim Hall
Graham Hill
Phil Hill
Al Holbert
Tony Hulman
Bobby Isaac
Ned Jarrett
Junior Johnson
Parnelli Jones

Niki Lauda
Fred Lorenzen
Tiny Lund
Rex Mays
John Marcum
Bruce McLaren
Rick Mears
Louie Meyer
Ralph Moody
Stirling Moss
Barney Oldfield
Wally Parks
Benny Parsons
David Pearson
Lee Petty
Richard Petty
Ferdinand Porsche
Eddie Rickenbacker

Fireball Roberts
Kenny Roberts
Mauri Rose
Johnny Rutherford
Wilbur Shaw
Carroll Shelby
Jackie Stewart
John Surtees
Herb Thomas
Mickey Thompson
Curtis Turner
Bobby Unser
Bill Vukovich
Rodger Ward
Joe Weatherly
Cale Yarborough
Smokey Yunick

For More Information

For Younger Readers

Benson, Michael. *Dale Earnhardt.* Broomall, PA: Chelsea House, 1996.

Frankl, Ron. *Richard Petty.* Broomall, PA: Chelsea House, 1996.

Hodges, David. *Classic Racing Cars.* Broomall, PA: Chelsea House, 1998.

Schleifer, Jay. *Indy: The Great American Race.* Worthington, OH: Silver Press, 1995.

Sullivan, George. *Burnin' Rubber: Behind the Scenes in Stock Car Racing.* Brookfield, CT: Millbrook Press, 1998.

Wukovits, John. *The Composite Guide to Auto Racing.* Broomall, PA: Chelsea House, 1998.

For Advanced Readers

Assael, Shaun. *Wide Open: Days and Nights on the NASCAR Tour.* New York: Ballantine Books, 1998.

Chapin, Kim. *Fast as White Lightning: The Story of Stock Car Racing,* rev. ed. New York: Random House, 1998.

Chimits, Xavier and Frances Granet. *Formula 1 Motor Racing Book: Renault F1.* New York: DK Pub., 1996.

Henry, Alan. *Wheel to Wheel: The Great Duels of Formula One Racing.* Ocseola, WI: Motorbooks International, 1996.

Isenberg, Hans Georg. *Great Racing Cars of the World.* Secaucus, NJ: Chartwell Books, 1994.

The Last Lap: The Life and Times of NASCAR's Legendary Heroes. Indianapolis: Macmillan General Reference, 1998.

NASCAR: The Thunder of America. New York: Harper Horizon, 1998.

Record, Melvyn. *High Octane: The Fastest Auto Racing Series.* Edison, NJ: Chartwell Books, 1995.

Rendal, Ivan. *The Checkered Flag: 100 Years of Motor Racing.* Secaucus, NJ: Chartwell Books, 1993.

Richardson, P.J. *Wheels of Thunder.* Nashville, TN: T. Nelson Publishers, 1997.

Wicker, Ned. *Indy Car C-H-A-M-P-I-O-N: A Season with Target/Chip Ganassi Racing.* Osceola, WI: Motorbooks, International, 1997.

Internet Sites

CART

http://www.cart.com/

Official site of the Championship Auto Racing Teams

Daytona International Speedway

http://www.nascar.com/winstoncup/tracks/daytona.html

Official site providing complete details on the historic track, including news about the Daytona 500.

Indianapolis 500

http://www.indy500.com/

Official site includes extensive history on the famed race and the Indianapolis Motor Speedway.

Motorsport News International

http://www.motorsport.com/

The motorsports site of record on the Internet. News, photos, and complete information on the top races and racers.

NASCAR

http://www.nascar.com/

Official site for the National Association for Stock Car Auto Racing.

National Hot Rod Association

http://www.nhraonline.com/

Complete news of the latest events and personalities in the world of hot-rod racing.

Index

Page numbers in *italics* indicate illustrations.

About the Author

Mark Stewart ranks among the busiest sportswriters of the 1990s. He has produced hundreds of profiles on athletes past and present and authored more than 40 books, including biographies of Jeff Gordon, Monica Seles, Steve Young, Hakeem Olajuwon, and Cecil Fielder. A graduate of Duke University, he is currently president of Team Stewart, Inc., a sports information and resource company located in Monmouth County, New Jersey.